# *22 Keys to Being a Minister*

# 22 Keys
# to Being
# a Minister

## (without Quitting
## or Wishing for
## Early Retirement)

## JAN G. LINN

CHALICE
PRESS
ST. LOUIS, MISSOURI

Bible quotations, unless otherwise noted, are from the *New Revised Standard Version Bible,* copyright 1989, Division of Christian Education of the National Council of the Churches of Christ in the United States of America. Used by permission. All rights reserved.

Cover photo: © D. Jeanene Tiner
Cover design: Elizabeth Wright
Interior design: Hui-chu Wang
Art director: Elizabeth Wright

This book is printed on acid-free, recycled paper.

Visit Chalice Press on the World Wide Web at
www.chalicepress.com

10   9   8   7   6   5   4   3   2   1          03   04   05   06   07

### Library of Congress Cataloging–in–Publication Data

Linn, Jan.
  22 keys to being a minister without quitting or wishing for early retirement / Jan G. Linn.—1st ed.
    p. cm.
  ISBN 0-8272-3645-X (alk. paper)
  1. Pastoral theology. 2. Clergy—Conduct of life. I. Title: Twenty-two keys to being a minister without quitting or wishing for early retirement. II. Title.
  BV4011.3.L56 2003
  253'.2—dc21

                                                    2003012262

Printed in the United States of America

# Contents

**Things to Know**

**What to Do When You Want to Quit Anyway**

# Acknowledgments

This book should have a second name on the cover: Joy Linn. She helped write it. It wasn't planned. We didn't decide to write a book together. No, she got hooked into it when I wrote the first draft and then asked her to read it. I do that with all my books, but this time the subject matter got to her. She has spent as many years in ministry as I have, in addition to being a PK (preacher's kid), which I am not. It was apparent after the first reading that she had a lot to say about what I was saying. In a few instances we didn't see eye to eye at all. In other places she cheered me on. In the end, the many and long hours we spent discussing the book evolved into a collaborative effort that bears the influence of each of us.

One of the graces given to writers is having people who do in fact read what you write with a critical eye, but all to the end that your work be better than it would otherwise be. Joy has done that several times. That her hand was in this one more than usual has increased its potential for offering clergy genuine encouragement and help. Indeed, without her urging after each reading that I rework one part or scrap another altogether, this material would not only be the lesser for it, but the challenge of addressing topics that matter to all of us who serve in ministry would have been greatly diminished. So to her I express my deepest gratitude for loving me and ministry too much to let what I write not have the best chance possible to build up ministers everywhere as they love and serve Christ's church here on earth.

Appreciation must also go to the folks at Chalice Press. They had no way of knowing how much this particular work meant to me at the time I proposed it. I did not even know myself. It was in the writing itself that the material came alive as it forced me to examine my own ministry at depths I had not before done. How others will judge the book is out of my hands, but when the last line was written, I knew that this was by far the most important work I have done. So thank you, David Polk, and all of you at Chalice Press. You do good and important work. The fact that I can be part of it is a privilege and personal blessing.

# Introduction
# (Why This Book)

First, a word to laity.

It is possible that you would enjoy reading this book, but in truth it was written for clergy. So if you are reading it now, it's probably because you found it lying on your minister's desk just like she wanted you to. But that's okay, because I want to say something to both of you about the title. It implies that the relationship between ministers and church members is adversarial. Well, it is. More than that, it has to be, not in the sense of open conflict, but in the tradition of biblical prophets who loved the people of Israel enough to tell them the truth. If your minister's sermons never make you uncomfortable, if in meetings she never challenges the direction the church is going or raises thorny questions about the priorities of the members, then either your minister doesn't know the gospel very well or your congregation has intimidated her into choosing to be a pastor without being a prophet. But if her sermons stir you up and if her comments in meetings have a way of stretching you in uncomfortable ways, then stop now and say a prayer of thanksgiving for the good minister God has sent your way.

You see, being a minister puts one in the unenviable position of serving as a representative of God to people who are always being tempted into idolatry. The people of Israel were. The Christians in the early church were. People today are no different. But I can tell you that this prophetic role your minister fulfills is far from easy. For one thing, he knows it is as difficult for him to live up to the demands of faithfulness as it is for you. In addition, his feet of clay make him more than a little insecure about upsetting you. After all, he likes to eat just like anyone else, and, if he has one, so does his family. So keep in mind that often the discomfort you feel after listening to a sermon (not all the time,

1

once in a while it may just be a bad sermon) comes from your
minister having the courage and integrity to speak the truth in
love.

Now to ministers.

This is not a book about leadership. It will touch on leadership
issues, but the primary subject is you. Specifically, it's about your
not only surviving as a minister, but enjoying being one. If you've
been doing ministry for more than twenty years, are you glad you
still are? If you're just out of seminary, do you find yourself
beginning to wonder if you want to do this the rest of your life?
These questions and others like them are the reason for this book.
There are many good books on leadership that can help you be a
success in whatever way the leadership book you might be reading
defines it. I happen to think that success in ministry is actually
simple enough for anyone to achieve. Do it with integrity, and
ground it in a deep spiritual life that nurtures your own faith.
Effectiveness may or may not be the fruit of integrity and spiritual
depth, but if you cannot look yourself in the mirror every
morning and feel good about what kind of minister you are, there
is no level of achievement that will make you a success.

But this book goes beyond any of that and offers some
suggestions that might help you serve your congregation without
wanting to throw in the towel. There are ministers serving all sizes
and kinds of churches who find themselves doing more and
enjoying it less. At the other end of the spectrum are those who
genuinely love what they are doing in places some would not want
to serve. What is absent in the former and the key to the latter is
staying alive spiritually. It is the hardest part of what we do. If you
already know how to do that, you probably don't need this book
(if you've already bought it, you might give it to someone who
does). But if you struggle with staying excited about your ministry
and your congregation, this book may help you reclaim your
spiritual heritage before you tell your people where to go even
though they haven't asked for directions.

One confession up front: What is written here is based as
much on learning from failures as from successes. The struggle not
only to do ministry but to enjoy it is as difficult for me as it is for
the next person. As far as I know, no one has a corner on truth,
and that includes how to be a minister in today's world of shallow

commitments and radical individualism. For better and for worse, those of us who are clergy are married to the church. Most of us have considered divorce, but having chosen to stay with it we need all the help we can get from one another. This book was written to do just that. Bear in mind, though, these are not 22 keys to being a success in ministry, or even being effective. They might help with both, but they also might not. What they will do is help you to be the kind of minister you need to be to do what you want to do without quitting or wishing for early retirement.

One final thing. I have a disdain for "steps to this" and "keys to that" kinds of books. I swore to myself that I would never write one. Moreover, I confess that there may be a bit of mischief in the book's title. But in the last few years I have come to realize that ministers for whom work has become a job are truly in need of some word that will help them regain their balance. I am the first to admit that there are no "keys" that can turn ministry around for someone who is ready to give up. But I am bold enough to say that these chapters do offer commonsense wisdom honed by more than a few years of experience—mine and others'—that just might help. Staying in ministry finally comes down to the person, but if this book encourages one good minister to keep going, it will have been worth the effort, no matter what the title is.

# Things to Remember

- Remember Who (Okay, Whom) You Work For
- Remember Who (Whom) You Go to Bed With
- Remember Why You Go to Work

# (1)

# Remember Who (Okay, Whom) You Work For

In a recent interview in the *Christian Century*, pastor/scholar Eugene Peterson was asked the question, "Many people think there's a crisis in ministry today, a crisis of morality or of morale. How do you see it?" He answered:

> I get the sense these days that many of my colleagues have external rewards in view. How do I become a good leader? How do I get published? How do I do this? How do I do that? Those are questions that are beside the point.

> We're not a market-driven church, and the ministry is not a market-driven vocation. We're not selling anything, and we're not providing goods and services. If a pastor is not discerning and discriminating about the claims of his or her vocation and about the claims of a congregation, then the demands or the desires of the congregation can dominate what he or she is doing and that creates the conditions for non-pastoral work.

> And then you can lose your morals and your morale because you're not working at anything that has any biblical order to it.[1]

That pretty much sums it up, doesn't it? Yet more than a few ministers today function as if external awards do matter. But for many, ministry has become a market-driven vocation, and their success is viewed as knowing how to sell. The fact that the "product" sold is services that churches offer is not anything about which to be encouraged. Too many churches have been turned into a service industry. How strange it is that Jesus talked so much about serving the needs of others while ministers are doing everything they can to meet the needs of church members. The call to service has been turned into service on demand.

A former German student at the seminary where I taught recently e-mailed me about his discouragement over having so little time to do ministry because of the services such as weddings, funerals, hospital visitation, and the like that he must provide to the people in the town where his church is located. The majority do not attend worship, but they pay church taxes to the state to get such services in return.

This predicament has not come to the U.S. in this form, but it does exist. It's not that weddings, funerals, and the like are not appropriate ministry. It is, instead, the fact that in many cases they top the list of congregational expectations of clergy while faith development and gospel proclamation are far down the list. Surveys suggest that the majority of people want spiritual nurture from their churches, yet decisions about joining a church are most often made on the basis of family wants and needs, which have virtually nothing to do with spiritual development and everything to do with services rendered and personal preferences satisfied. The situation for mainline churches limited in resources and personnel has gotten more difficult because of the growing development of Christian mega-mart churches that provide services ranging from health clubs to on-site fishing. Since overall church attendance in this country has not changed significantly in the last fifteen years, hovering somewhere between twenty-five and forty percent, it is obvious that mega-mart churches are growing at the expense of others. "Switching" is a more accurate description of the reason for their growth than conversion.

Not long ago the mother of a family in our church decided to seek out a church with more children the age of her own adolescents. Ironically, at the very time the family made this decision we gained two new families who have several foster children the ages of this woman's children. But the significant part of this story is that the church she chose is one her husband says has a theology personally offensive to him. That he is willing to expose his children to a perspective on faith he does not want for himself, all because his wife wants them to be with a few more children their age, suggests that, at least in today's "faith market," faith issues can be less important than "market" concerns.

This situation is not lost on clergy, who feel compelled to do whatever is feasible to meet the needs of church members. Perhaps that is why Peterson went on to comment:

> If you look at the numbers and money, American churches in some ways are the most successful churches ever. And yet I think it could be argued, we're at probably one of the lowest points because of the silliness and triviality that characterize so much of church life these days.[2]

A market-driven church is bound to end up in silliness and triviality. Yet clergy are often found leading the way in order to keep the people they have or have any hope of getting new ones. None of us is immune to this kind of pressure. The key to resisting it lies in remembering the One to whom we are ultimately accountable. It is not the church board, the lay leadership cabinet, or the new family that makes a visit to Sunday worship. It is God Almighty! The only true God. There are other things people make into gods. But there is only one God Almighty, only One who is worthy of our devotion and obedience, only One to whom we are finally accountable. The apostle Paul advises the Christians at Rome to live a life that pleases God (Rom. 12:1). He is the One we should seek to please. No one and nothing else are deserving of this kind of loyalty.

This is a good word to all of us who are clergy. It is easy to get caught up in the work of ministry and lose sight of the One whom we are seeking to please. God is the One we work for. Ministers don't work for the church. Ministers don't work for the denomination. Ministers don't work for the community at large. Ministers work for God. To use workplace language, God is our employer. It is God's view of what we do that matters most. Faithfulness to God may not fill the pews on Sunday, but it does fill the soul of clergy with a sense of worth and dignity. More than that, it gives us the kind of inward freedom without which ministry cannot be done with genuine joy or, at times, integrity.

In his book *Unlearning Church,* Michael Slaughter confesses that he "wrongly bought into the pastor-as-CEO model during the 1990's and forgot that I am to be a spiritual guide and coach."[3] He is to be commended for this candid admission, but the question that immediately came to mind when I read what he wrote is, "How did he ever think being a minister meant being a CEO?" How could any minister who knows the New Testament witness to both Jesus and the faith of the early church confuse clergy leadership with the position of a CEO? The answer, I believe, is as simple as it is profound. Michael Slaughter forgot the One he worked for. He let a booming church life cloud his vision of what the church is. As a result, he reached for the thing he thought might equip him to do the best he could by his people. In doing so he was not able to do his best by God. But I cannot be too hard on him. The rest of us are more like him than we are different. He at least had the courage to admit his mistake. Moreover, he did so while still riding the tide of external success.

Ministry is born of God. This is the most important thing we can learn as we begin in ministry, and the one thing we can ill afford to forget as the years pass. We are human beings bearing the awesome responsibility of speaking for God to our people and making petitions on their behalf to God. Weekly many of us join our people in praying, "Your kingdom come; Your will be done; on earth as it is in heaven." For clergy these words remind us of whom we work for. They tell us what it is that we are supposed to be doing. We are about "kingdom work." The fact that it is "on earth" does not change where our loyalty lies.

Seeing clergy lead their church to understand and practice such loyalty is a thing of beauty these days. Several years ago a new church in my own denomination was started by a pastor who from the beginning had a vision of a congregation that was intentionally welcoming of all persons, irrespective of sexual preference. Church consultants would have said at the time that this was a direction of certain death for this new church. Today, however, it is a thriving and growing congregation led by a minister who in terms of her understanding of the gospel has not forgotten the

One she works for, and it is clear that she is having the time of her life in ministry. There are similar stories of ministers whose theological perspective is opposite from that of the minister above, but the result is the same. A Baptist minister friend does ministry with great integrity and courageous leadership. We talk often about the struggles of today's pastor, but even on the most trying days this man has an obvious passion for ministry. That is the way it is when we remember whom we work for. We are filled with a sense of satisfaction in the midst of the struggles we face.

What I know better today than I knew years ago is that remembering the One I work for is how I am able to continue doing what I am doing. The churches I have served have disappointed me as much as I have them. And being a leader in the church makes disappointments all the more hurtful because we are part of a divine work that involves changing the world. How could it not be discouraging when clergy see members of the body of Christ treating discipleship as something to do whenever they can find the time? It is in precisely these moments that remembering that our work is God's work is essential It is what helps us keep our balance and weigh disappointments against those moments when we see church members do their best to live up to the high calling that is theirs in Jesus Christ.

When Elizabeth O'Connor first wrote about the Church of the Savior in Washington, D.C., a special community of faith whose story inspired a generation of hopeful clergy during some difficult days in the life of both the church and the nation, she said that they had learned two things early in their life together: (1) "Work which is worth doing is never done without great sacrifice," and (2) "A dream is not without difficult times—times when those who work with it are discouraged and when it seems those who were committed to it have lost the vision."[4] Every minister knows how true both these observations are. They are the reason we must always remember whom we work for as ministers of the gospel. Regardless of the extent to which churches get caught up in silliness and lose themselves in trivialities, we work for God Almighty, and those whose souls are entrusted into our care belong to the Same!

Saying this, though, certainly doesn't make it happen. Remembering whom we work for is born of the Spirit. Without attending to our spiritual life, clergy are bound to be consumed by daily demands that make us forget whose we are. Preaching about and teaching others to attend to spiritual needs without doing it ourselves certainly rings hollow, but worse is the "hollowness" that grows in us. Remembering whom we work for is the work of the Holy Spirit, a union of mind and heart devoted to loving Jesus as well as serving his church. The ever-present danger in ministry is spiritual aridity, in which we do our work simply because it's our job. If you've been in ministry for a while, you know what this experience is like. All of us go through it. If it persists, however, it can be devastating, because spiritual strength gives memory its power. Remembering is as much about devotion as it is about thinking. We think about the people we love, but we don't always love the people we think about. There is no way one can continue to do ministry if it involves the latter, and there is no way one cannot if it is grounded in the former.

# (2)

## Remember Who (Whom)
## You Go to Bed With

"Why Do Pastors Quit Their Posts?" was a study done in 2001 by the Indianapolis-based Pastors Institute. It found that as many as 1,400 clergy leave their positions each month, either on a temporary basis or permanently. Twelve reasons emerged as the primary causes, a mixed bag of factors with which most ministers can identify. They were ranked as follows:

1 Felt resigning was the best way out
2 Disillusioned over church's spiritual condition
3 Fatigue or burnout
4 Influenced by denominational leaders
5 Needed more income
6 Pastoring was no longer a ministry
7 Influenced by spouse or relative
8 Lost interest in pastoring
9 Terminated by congregation
10 Felt inadequate or unprepared
11 Transferred to another church ministry
12 Poor health

The body of the report also reveals something all ministers know to be true: One's spouse can play a significant role in any decision to leave or return to ministry. While influence from a spouse (or relative) ranked only seventh in the overall survey as a factor in leaving ministry, when asked if one's spouse supported a return to ministry, 57 percent of the respondents said no. Yet 65 percent said they miss pastoring, and 59 percent responded that they hoped to return to it.[1]

Tension in parsonage marriages because of ministry has a long history in the Protestant tradition. Congregational expectations of both clergy and their families can be unrealistic and possessive. In addition, there is the "glass house" effect that makes the Orwellian eye of Big Brother a common experience for clergy families. It is quite unsettling to know that you cannot escape the watchfulness of other people, even when they care about you. A little privacy is everybody's need.

One would think that the divorce rate among clergy, or the mere fact of clergy divorce, would be an obvious sign of spousal conflict over ministry, but this may not in fact be the case. The causes of divorce are almost always multiple and often unknown by those involved in it. Sometimes the real causes of divorce are not understood until years after the fact. It would be unusual for ministry to be the lone contributor. It is possible that clergy who divorce are in marriages that would likely end the same way were ministry not a factor. But whatever the reason, troubled clergy marriages are a reminder that for married clergy the most important human relationship we have is with the person we sleep with every night. Relationships are where the gospel is played out in daily life. In order to preach and teach this message with passion and confidence, we who do ministry must know in our minds and feel in our hearts that the relationship we have with the person we live with is reliable. This is the person we need to feel we can go to when we need a friend, when we are troubled, when we wonder if what we are doing is worth doing anymore.

It should be obvious why this is the case. Spouses are the people who know those of us who are ministers most intimately. One of my professors once remarked that it was a sobering thought when he stood in the pulpit to look out at his wife and realize that she might be thinking, "This is the man I have sex with." These many years later I am beginning to understand the significance of his comment. A spouse is the person who sees naked the person whom others call pastor. She is the one who knows just how unsure and vulnerable the one preaching the gospel often feels. He is the one who knows her bathroom habits and what she looks like when she wakes up in the morning. Spouses set the tone for every other relationship a minister has. They are the people we should know the best. Taking for granted the relationship we share with the person we sleep with can be fatal to ministry as well as to the marriage. Ironically, the fact that we are clergy makes us even more vulnerable to neglecting this core relationship. Ministry involves people problems on a daily basis. We eat, drink, and sleep people issues. Thus, relationships easily become work, and before we realize it, we are looking to home as a refuge from it. Energy for our own marriage can be siphoned by those whose lives have demanded our attention. Then guilt debilitates us all the more as we realize that communication, time for each other, and attending to the little things—all of which we tell couples they must do to save their marriage—we cannot do for ourselves.

It's a simple thing really. Married clergy need a good marriage if we are to enjoy ministry. Experience bears out that there is a direct corollary between happiness in marriage and fulfillment in ministry. Indeed, I believe it is actually sequential. The latter depends on the former. This is not to say that fulfillment in ministry depends on one's being married, only that this is true for ministers who are married. No day in ministry can be what it could be if at its end we don't want to go home. Unfortunately it sometimes takes the actual experience for us to understand how true this is. By then, of course, it may be too late.

An important dimension of remembering whom we sleep with is good sex. Not the kind of sex we see in movies or read about in novels. Good sex involves much more than the sexual act. It is about intimacy, about delighting in giving as much as receiving, about loving to love each other. This kind of sex is an emotional bonding, a way of sharing ourselves with another we trust with our lives. It is intimacy that speaks of the absence of the fear of being exposed. Good sex involves a nakedness of the soul that makes one feel safe in the midst of total vulnerability. Good sex is person-centered rather than performance-centered. It has the power to make partners feel as if they are participating in a sacred act because their being together in this way is an expression of a sacred trust born of their common bond with God.

American culture has diminished the beauty and gift of sex by making it a purely physical act, turning it into a self-centered pursuit of pleasure where the need to be fulfilled overshadows the desire to fulfill and performing well replaces sharing well. The result is momentary satisfaction rather than enduring affection. Sex in American culture is the ultimate expression of the superficial, solipsistic society we have become. Obviously, the parsonage marriage bed needs to be something more than this if clergy are to experience the power of married life that contributes to one's joy in ministry.

It is tempting for ministers to place responsibility for this kind of intimacy on spouses. This expectation becomes even more convoluted when the couple are both clergy, as is the case in my own marriage. Yet a moment's reflection on the meaning of marriage points to what we all know to be true: Attending to all aspects of any relationship is a mutual responsibility. Remembering whom we sleep with is no exception. At the same time, this fact underscores the connection between good sex and all the other aspects of the marriage being good. Good sex is not possible when two people share little else that is good between them. Thus, remembering whom we sleep with is a call to give the time and energy required for our clergy marriage to be a good one.

This should not take any of us by surprise. We are the ones who tell people that what Scott Peck wrote in his book *The Road Less Traveled* is true: Love is more than a feeling and requires hard work to be enduring.[2] That is precisely why it *is* the road less traveled. Yet so many people, clergy included, want to get love the same way they want to get other things: free and easy. Ironically, because ministers talk constantly about loving others, we can easily fall into the trap of romanticizing love and resisting the work it requires in our own home. But in the real world of love and hate, working to love the person we sleep with is the only chance we have at intimacy. Every husband and wife face this choice.

It is amazingly easy in ministry to give ourselves to everything but our own marriage. It can be a fatal mistake not only for our marriage, but for our ministry. Neglect in marriage will likely lead to a sense of failure in ministry as well. Sins of omission have this kind of impact because we know they are preventable. Sins of commission are not excusable, but they are understandable.

Human beings are imperfect. But this logic breaks down when it comes to the failure to do what we could have done if we had the forethought to do it. The human element is less compelling in its ability to assuage guilt in situations where an omission is at fault. This is precisely what neglect is: an omission, a failure to be present when we could have, a failure to give time and energy we could have given.

But beyond any of this, neglecting our marriage relationship means missing an opportunity to enjoy the most filling and fulfilling of all human relationships. Even the British skeptic Bertrand Russell once remarked that under the appropriate conditions marriage offered human beings their greatest chance for happiness. To go home to a happy relationship when the day is done is a key factor for clergy wanting to get up the next morning to go to work. That certainly makes remembering whom we sleep with worth it.

# (3)

# Remember Why You Go to Work

Speaking of going to work, it is important to remember why you do. The word is *vocation*. Ministers go to work because we are called by God to go. There is no room for ambiguity here. Clarity is essential. Doubts about call can easily lead to a loss of focus. When that happens, ministry becomes a job with high stress and low pay. But as a holy calling it is a privileged opportunity that one is humbled to be offered.

A former colleague has written eloquently about seeing the whole of life as a vocation. He writes:

> To speak of vocation is to talk about what it means to be human, the purposes for which we live and the ends toward which we move. This is the fundamental promise of each newborn child to the world. From cradle to grave, in different periods of life as youth or adults, parents or children, friends or lovers, we embody a variety of roles and responsibilities, and we must live through different kinds of situations and circumstances. By and large others see us partially, that is, what we are for them. But what calls us forth is that which names us, that which we are that no one else is.[1]

Later in the same article he makes the observation: "Vocation is the sense of our lives as a gift and life as a mystery whose purpose, though never fully comprehended, is revealed in the diverse ways to each of us."[2]

His words remind us that life is much more than one thing after another, that what we do in life is an extension of who we are. At the same time, this does not lessen the significance of "special callings" that claim a person for a specific work to be done. Such is the call to ministry. It is nothing less than the call to do the Lord's bidding. The content of this bidding is not in question. Our work is to preach the gospel of Jesus Christ. This is our vocation. It is our calling. It is what we do if we are to do ministry. Everything we do must be directed toward the goal of making Jesus known in the world. Without this sense of vocation you will find it harder and harder to get up and go to work in the real world of ministry.

For several years I served as a member of the admissions committee of the seminary where I taught. Every applicant visited campus and met separately with each member of the committee before any action was taken. In all those years I do not recall more than a handful of applicants who described their reason for entering ministry in language that could be deciphered into anything close to wanting to preach the gospel. Most of the time it was because they wanted to help people or they hoped one day to become a college or seminary teacher. For these potential ministers the question of vocation had been reduced to caring for others or realizing a professional goal, neither of which is a bad thing, but both lack the power to sustain one in ministry.

What I am talking about, of course, is having a passion for the Christian gospel. This is what a sense of vocation means in ministry. Such passion today, though, is often looked on with suspicion out of concern for religious intolerance, of which Christians have been and continue to be guilty. But respect for diversity is no excuse for a lack of commitment to and passion for telling the story of Jesus. As clergy this is our message, and telling it is our life's vocation. Anything less than a passion to make Jesus known in the world will serve neither the cause of Christ nor a decision to enter ministry. There are many ways to help people and many subjects to teach, but being in ministry means serving as an ambassador for Jesus Christ (2 Cor. 5:20). Nothing can substitute for this commitment if vocational integrity is to be maintained.

The key, of course, is in believing the gospel ourselves. Passion is not possible without it. It is here that I am convinced clergy are most vulnerable. The combination of years of study and discouragement over church conflict can cause ministers to lose hope that the gospel can actually change people's lives. Add to this the sense of our own personal failures in faithful discipleship, and ministry slips silently into work to do rather than a vocation to fulfill. Daily responsibilities become chores to be carried out. It is true that ministry always involves doing things none of us wants to do, but the line between job and vocation is crossed at the moment these tasks lose their connection to proclaiming the Lord we are called to serve.

The above inevitably happens when ministers lose sight of what is ultimately at stake in what they are doing. Lives are at stake when we speak or act in the name of Jesus. Getting bogged down in church work instead of doing the work of the church is not only a sign of a loss of vision that leads to weariness in ministry, it is downright dangerous. In a world where people are dying— whether literally or from meaninglessness—turning ministry into church work constitutes a vocational betrayal of epic proportions.

To save the world is why clergy go to work. For more than one reason the world is in fact "going to hell in a handbasket." We share with all Christians the urgent task of making known the good news that God loves the world too much to let this happen and sent Jesus to prove it. Daily we have the opportunity to teach others the way that leads to life, inviting them to partner with one another in working out their own salvation (Phil. 2:12) in the ways Jesus taught (as, for example, in the Sermon on the Mount).

No parable speaks a relevant word to clergy today more than that of the prodigal son. Both brothers are suffering from their failure to understand what it means to be a son. Each represents the unchurched and churched of today. Within and outside the communities of faith where we minister, people are suffering because they do not know what being a child of God means for their lives, or even that they are children of God. These people are lost: a category mainline clergy don't speak much about anymore. But its importance remains nonetheless. To be lost, as Dallas Willard writes, means to be out of place. And as he goes on to point out, being out of place is to be useless. The New Testament word *Gehenna,* he says, can be understood as the place for the useless. Willard then uses the helpful analogy of a set of keys to make his point. Lost keys are simply useless, not because they are bad or defective, but because they are lost. That is the human condition. The vocation of minister is to tell people where the keys are.[3] Once a minister realizes what is at stake in preaching the gospel, the desire to do ministry grows rather than diminishes with every passing year. Passion builds. The urgency of one's calling takes over.

Mainline clergy today face the task of rescuing the language of faith from an offensive Christian fundamentalism that thrives on "us" and "them" categories. Caught off guard by their appeal to many Christians within our churches, we took flight to a world of "I'm okay; you're okay" inclusivity that refuses to speak of anyone being "saved" and "lost." In the process we left the prodigal in his pigsty and the elder brother without a clue as to how to enjoy the family reunion. In short, we failed to take the human brokenness we claimed to be concerned about seriously enough to be upset by it. When a person searching for meaning or caught in self-destructive behavior is simply a minister's next counseling appointment, the fire for ministry has all but gone out.

Nothing about ministry on a daily basis can motivate clergy to want to do what we do except that all of it expresses the ache we carry deep inside to share Jesus with others who are lost and need to be found. To use biblical metaphors that speak of reality, life here on earth holds potential for either heaven or hell. That it matters which one people choose to experience is why we do what we do in ministry. It is the one thing that will always get us up in the morning, ready and anxious to work.

A good practice for clergy is to remember the day we felt God tap us for this service, or the moment when the meaning of the "holy" nudges we were feeling became clear. It is this remembering that can renew our zeal for that which is the greatest privilege one can be granted: to do the Lord's bidding. If this practice does not inspire you afresh to go to work, it may be time for you to stay in bed. But if the fires of your vocation are rekindled, you will have little difficulty greeting the next day of your ministry.

# Things Not to Do

- Don't Pretend to Know More Than You Do
- Don't Let People Who Let You Down, Get You Down
- Don't Overestimate Your Importance
- Don't Undervalue Your Influence
- Don't Hesitate to Apologize
- Don't Be Afraid to Put Your Cards on the Table
- Don't Idealize Motivation
- Don't Try to Leap Tall Buildings in a Single Bound
- Don't Be a Stranger to Your Children

# (4)

# Don't Pretend to Know More
# Than You Do

No minister would admit to making this mistake, yet there are those in whose hands knowledge becomes a dangerous thing. In a manner of speaking it gives them "gas," a "puffed up" condition the New Testament suggests is a barrier to spiritual growth (1 Cor. 13:4, KJV). These ministers focus on what they know to the exclusion of what they don't, ironically revealing how much more they need to know. Others pretend to know more than they do for the opposite reason. They know they don't know much but are afraid church members will find out. The rest of us stand in between these extremes, but still manage to make this mistake from time to time mainly because we don't recognize that this is what we are doing.

A reliable sign of this condition among ministers is the propensity for offering what I call "stained-glass" answers to complex and perplexing matters. "Stained-glass" answers sound pious, explain little, and sometimes make for very poor theology. The father of a member of a church that I was serving died unexpectedly while in the hospital for what the family thought was a minor problem. The father was not young but had no medical reason not to expect to live several more years. Naturally, his death shocked his family. I was asked to share leadership in the funeral service with a more seasoned minister of another church. Having little experience in ministry, I was more than happy to do so. What made a lasting impression on me was the fact that even though this pastor did not know the father very well, he spoke of him and his death as if he possessed intimate knowledge of both. "We need not weep," he said to me and the son of the man who had died, "Dad Stansbury was ready to go. He was ready to go." (These many years later his exact words remain vivid.) I remember wondering how he knew that and what "ready to go" meant to him. He didn't know, of course, but he thought he needed to speak as if he did.

Ministers may think they need to appear knowledgeable on all fronts, but it's a good bet church members don't. They are content to hear ministers tell all the truth they know without trying to tell all the truth there is. Church members can recognize the absence of authenticity in the brightest of clergy. The minister who admits to honest struggle in matters of faith and refuses to pretend that difficult questions yield easy answers is a person to whom laity who struggle and question in the same ways can relate. This is a good thing because the nature of our vocation is to raise questions and avoid simple answers. Only the minister who fears vulnerability will try to hide these struggles.

The minister who feels the need to appear to know more than he does diminishes being taken seriously when he speaks of that which he actually does know. Ministers ought to possess a great deal of knowledge appropriate for effective leadership. Laity need counsel and guidance from clergy who have been educated to provide it. It is the nature of our "equipping ministry" that the apostle Paul wrote about (Eph. 4:12). Laity rightly expect us to know more than they know theologically, and we should not be hesitant to be assertive in those moments when we can bring more to the table than they can. Speaking out of turn, however, about mysteries such as unexpected death, innocent suffering, natural disasters, and good and evil undermines credibility when it is most needed.

September 11, 2001, is a watershed moment in American history that more than any modern event helped to bring focus to the need for clergy not to speak beyond their knowledge or understanding. It is encouraging that many have shown remarkable restraint in speaking about those moments that shocked the world. The insights of Rabbi Brad Hirshfield, who was one of several interviewed for the PBS program *Faith and Doubt at Ground Zero*,[1] shown one year after 9/11, are especially helpful in understanding why in such circumstances restraint often serves the cause of faith better than quick and careless explanations. The interviewer asked, "Have people asked you where God was on September 11? How do you answer that?" Rabbi Hirshfield responded:

> Yes, since September 11, people keep asking me, "Where was God?" And they think because I'm a rabbi that I have answers. There is a part of me that wants to yell back at them, "What? You're asking now? Why now? Why didn't you ask about Bosnia or Rwanda or Hiroshima or gas chambers and concentration camps or go back through all of human history? I don't understand. Now you're asking 'Where was God?' How many people go to bed hungry every night in the richest country in the world? And now you're asking about 'Where is the God of justice?'"
>
> I don't mean to demean their question; so I always have to kind of check myself; go back and try and understand. What they are looking for is what all of us are looking for: some way to let real life, with the pain, not blow us apart—probably a bad use of terms. We're all looking for that. I guess the most important part of that conversation is to begin to identify how all of us are looking for that real life, rather than use some notion of God or some doctrine or some religion to provide easy answers, when we know deep down that they don't really exist. So I can make someone feel good for ten minutes doing the stuff I don't believe, but I know, and they know, that ten minutes later, the same questions come flooding back. I actually think that my job as a rabbi is to help them live with those questions.

The interviewer then asked, "Isn't it fair for people to have a hope that [there] might be [a God of justice], in other words, the image of a God [who intervenes]?" Rabbi Hirshfield again responded:

I don't think hoping for God to intervene is childlike or naive. I think it's actually quite compelling, and I think, at some level, I really feel that. But it's so hard, because the people flying those airplanes thought God was intervening, too. So it's not that you shouldn't hope for it. But you have to understand how that hope can be used to justify both that which is most nurturing and most horrific.

Some people who made it out of the World Trade Center say with great militancy, "God saved me." But what about the other 3,000 people? Have you encountered this? Yes, sure. As long as you can really feel that "God saved me" without feeling that God didn't save them, then I think it's a beautiful belief.

When people come and say, "I feel I was saved by God because my wife called me and sent me to the market," this is a real story. Someone calls me and explains to me, "I was saved by God on September 11. My wife called me and reached me before Metro North. She asked if, when I got on the subway to go downtown, I could stop and do an errand. That was the hand of God."

And it's like, yes! But now what do you say to the person who's the wife who didn't call the husband, or the husband who didn't call the wife, and who now just has a photograph and not even a body to bury? That God didn't love them? That they were being punished for some sin? See, it's not that I want people to give up on the feeling that "God saved me." I have felt that in my own life, and I love that feeling. I think that you have to just be careful how you look at the people who God didn't save, so to speak. That's the problem. It's not that it's bad to feel we've been saved by God and feel grateful and feel blessed. It's just, how do you look at the people who didn't have that experience? And subtly or not so subtly, are you communicating that they're less blessed, they're less loved, they're less religious?

So it's not that I mind people feeling saved by God when it breaks right; it's the hubris that comes in for the people for whom it doesn't happen that scares me. If we can figure out a way to feel absolutely blessed and loved by God when it breaks right, without looking at other people and saying, "Oh well, they're cursed because they're not good enough, loved enough, religious enough," whatever the language will be. I want to be in close connection to that personal God. But that personal God also justifies a lot of nastiness.

At this point Rabbi Hirshfield makes a suggestion as to how rabbis and ministers can answer people who have serious questions to ask.

If God's ways are mysterious, then don't tell me about the plan. Live with the mystery. It's upsetting; it's scary; it's painful; it's deep; it's rich; and it's interesting—but no plan. That's what mystery is. It's all of those things. You want plan? Then tell me about plan. But if you're going to tell me about how the plan saved you, you'd better also be able to explain how the plan killed them. And the test of that has nothing to do with saying it in your synagogue or your church. The test of that has to do with going and saying it to the person who just buried someone and look in their eyes and tell them, "God's plan was to blow your loved one apart." Look at them and tell them that God's plan was that their children should go to bed every night for the rest of their lives without a parent. If you can say that, well, at least you're honest. I don't worship the same God. But that at least has integrity. But it's too easy. That's my problem with the answer. Not that I think they're being inauthentic when people say it or being dishonest; it's just too damn easy.

The honesty Rabbi Hirshfield models in his responses points to the folly of anyone, especially those who supposedly speak for God, speaking of things not given to them to know. Faith does not require knowledge of all things to be strong. More than anything it requires love, enough love to tell people the truth. And in truth speaking we can witness to the mystery of faith, the mystery of believing in a good God when bad things happen to innocent people. It will serve people better to do this than to pretend to know more than we do. It will also free us to tell what we do know with credibility and confidence.

Speaking freely, but not carelessly or presumptuously, is one way clergy are good stewards of the role we play in the lives of church members. They look to us in their most difficult and vulnerable moments. To know that we have been faithful to this privilege with words that go far enough to comfort but not so far as to explain the inexplicable has great power to make ministry seem worthwhile. Other things may have gone wrong, but on those days when we know we have served as a good pastor to someone in need, we go home with a deep sense that what we do truly matters.

But we also believe that we have served the cause of Christ in a larger way. These days, when skepticism is common and the church's authority is questioned without hesitation, matters of life and death must be addressed in a way that has credibility. Ministers can serve this purpose, and when we do a feeling of satisfaction is born in us that not even the harshest criticism can take away. Most of us will never be among the movers and shakers of the world, but moments do come our way when we have the chance to speak and act in a manner that does justice to the gospel. There is no greater reward in ministry when this happens, and no stronger motivation to stay the course.

# (5)

# Don't Let People Who Let You Down, Get You Down

Every minister has church members she can count on: people she knows will be there when she needs them, people whose support is unwavering even when she makes a misstep. But the rest of the story is that there are others who have been the source of her deepest frustrations and worst disappointments. These are the polarities between which every minister lives and moves. The fact that it is so common would lead us to think that ministers know how to cope with it. Some do. Increasingly, though, more and more do not. The people who let them down, get them down, and once they do, it is a daunting task to climb out of the hole.

One reason ministers get knocked down is because we believe the best about people. We take them at their word and are ready to count on them when they say they will do something. What we forget is that they are people with good intentions who, like us, do not always have sufficient commitment to follow through. Just when we need them the most, they let us down. That part is their fault. But when they get us down, that part is our fault. It is important for ministers to make this distinction, lest we fall into holding regular "ain't it awful" pity parties.

This struggle to keep our head is easily exacerbated when clergy take disappointments personally. It is a tendency with which I contend on a regular basis. It has always felt like a personal rejection when people quit a church I am serving or work against

31

an idea I propose. It may not be my fault—and in my experience it usually isn't—but most of the time it feels like it is, and that hurts. New-church ministry is especially susceptible to this. New churches are a constant ebb and flow of people who stay for a while and then leave, generally for reasons known only to them.

On the day we remembered the events of 9/11 a man attended our worship service for the first time. It went as well as it could have. People seemed genuinely touched, and more than one thanked me for the sermon, something that seldom happens among stoic Minnesotans. The next day we followed our usual practice and left a loaf of homemade bread at the man's door with a letter inviting him to visit us again. The following morning there was a message on the church's answering machine from him. He thanked us for what he described as "absolutely delicious bread," commented on how much he enjoyed the worship service, and then in so many words said that he would not be coming back.

I remember sitting in my chair listening to his message several times, getting more and more angry. It would have been funny had it not been so upsetting. A person attends worship, thinks the service was excellent (his words), is appreciative of the hospitality shown to him, and then says he won't be coming back. Did I take it personally? You bet. Did I feel discouraged? Absolutely.

Then I asked Joy to listen to his message. Afterwards she made the almost offhand comment, "Well, for goodness' sake." That was it. I couldn't believe she was taking it so lightly. If she was disappointed, she didn't show it. I knew she wasn't discouraged in the least. When I asked why it didn't upset her, she said, "Because we did all we could do. The service was great. The bread said 'We hope you will come back.' That's all we can do. I guess we're not the kind of church he's looking for."

She was right. We must not have been, but I wanted to find him and say, "What do you mean we're not the kind of church you're looking for? You would be damned lucky to be in a church like ours." But I eventually got hold of my emotions and realized that Joy's was an example of how to be let down without getting down. It's not all that complicated to figure out. We choose not to, and we make that choice because we don't want other people to have that kind of control over us. The minute I started letting this man's actions get me down, I was handing my head to him on a silver platter. Not that he wanted it. He had no desire to hurt me or our church. He didn't set out to disappoint us. That was all my doing. Naturally, his choice not to come back was a letdown, but it was my choice alone to let it get me down.

One way to fight this temptation to get down is to develop the mental habit of thinking about the people we actually can count on. For everyone who lets us down, there is someone else who picks us up. In this instance it was my wife, but it could just as well have been others in our congregation who are giving time and energy and money to make this ministry go. But disappointments have the power of making these people invisible when we bow to it. In better moments ministers know that when we allow the people who let us down to get us down, we let down the very people we can count on. It becomes a negative circle that damages the spirit of minister and laity alike.

This entire book is focused on what clergy can do to avoid getting down so far that we want to give up. Each of these suggestions offers a choice, but at the end of the day that is what staying in ministry is: a choice. In reality, it is the kind of choice that is a composite of numerous other ones along the way that make us vulnerable to discouragement. Ministers cannot avoid being disappointed. The alternative is simply to stop caring about people, something we obviously cannot and do not want to do. In light of the nature of our calling, we have to choose to focus either on the people we can count on or the people who have demonstrated that we cannot, a choice for either staying up or getting down.

To make the healthy choice involves letting go of those who may have already let us down. Otherwise, we keep them ever present by fixating on what they did to hurt or disappoint us. It was during a recent weekend silent retreat with church members that I recognized this tendency in myself. A short time into the silence I found my mind focused on some couples who had left our church at a time when their continued participation could have helped us turn an important corner in getting fully established as a new church. Each had what they believed were good reasons for leaving, and none left angry or bitter. But Joy and I believe even now that all of them could have chosen to stay for at least another year without making any major sacrifice (three of them moved away but not with job transfers). They, of course, saw it a different way. On the retreat I was confronted with the anger I had been carrying around about their decisions. It was evident that the Spirit was telling me to let it go, that I was fighting discouragement because I was hanging on to the disappointment I felt. I journaled about what I was feeling, and then I went into the chapel at the retreat center and prayed the hurt away. It was as simple as that—though, of course, it wasn't simple at all.

Ministers, of course, are not the only people who struggle with not letting people who let you down, get you down. As strange as it may seem, the group clergy might learn the most from is police. These are people who literally put their lives on the line for the sake of others. Many times they get out of bed and go to work when only the day before a court system let a known criminal go free on a technicality. The system may have to function this way to protect everyone's rights, but that doesn't soften the devastating disappointment police experience when, for example, that system puts someone such as a repeated sex offender back on the street to claim another victim. Some officers choose to become embittered. A few choose to make the law rather than enforce it. The majority go back to their jobs in the hope that next time their work will not be in vain. It all comes down to choice.

Make no mistake, refusing to give in to the impulse to give up is difficult. But it is also worth it, and it is one we who serve in ministry can make. It is, in fact, the choice we must make in order to have the chance once in a while to make a real difference in someone's life. And when we do, we quickly come to understand that in ministry there is simply too much at stake to allow people who let us down, get us down.

# (6)

# Don't Overestimate Your Importance

In light of the discussion in the previous chapter, you would think that overestimating our importance is not a temptation for clergy. But not so fast. The issue is not how we think about laity. It's how we think about ourselves. The apostle Paul advised, "[Do not] think of yourself more highly than you ought to think" (Rom. 12:3b), but it's a temptation for ministers, not because ministers are a conceited bunch, but because of the position we occupy. We are leaders. We are up front. We are in charge. We have a weekly audience. We serve on important boards and agencies. We write books. We are invited to speak at special occasions. These are the things that go with leadership. But they also contain the seeds of our undoing when we get so full of ourselves that we fill up every room we walk into.

Leaders' thinking of themselves more highly than they should is dangerous because of the power available to them. In politics, wars get started this way. In government, citizen welfare and rights get trampled on. In business, workers are treated unjustly, stock holders get ripped off, and consumers are lied to. In ministry, people are manipulated to satisfy ego needs. Leaders always have power, some more than others, but the nature of leadership is that some measure of power is always at our disposal. How it is used will depend in part on the way the leader views herself. Power in the hands of anyone who thinks of herself more highly than is appropriate means power will be corrupting.

The first victim of corrupting power is conscience. The person who believes his own press clippings has lost touch with his moral center. "Right" and "wrong" become abstract categories easily pushed aside in the real world of winning and losing. Personal achievement becomes the chief goal. Once conscience is gone, everything else falls like dominoes: concern for others, responsibility to the whole, attentiveness to mission, lifting up the achievement of others, and teamwork. The whole gamut of communal values and personal integrity will have been sacrificed. The only thing left is the ego of the leader who has sacrificed everyone and everything else for the sake of personal importance. This should not happen anywhere, but we all know it does. It definitely should never happen in the church, but we all know that it does anyway. It doesn't usually happen in such dramatic fashion as to bring down the house, but overestimating our importance can and does undercut ministry. Someone once remarked that a package is never so small as a man wrapped up in himself. All of us in ministry— women and men—will serve God and the church better if we keep this in mind.

Two contrasting stories make this point. A clergy colleague attended a conference at a well-known megachurch. During a meal break he saw the pastor of the hosting church sitting at a table alone. His address had raised some questions in my colleague's mind regarding the transportability of the model the minister had described to settings different from that of a megachurch, so he sat down at the table in hopes of discussing them. Instead of welcoming this inquiry, however, the minister made a curt and rude response and at one point, when others began to sit down, physically turned his back to this colleague, who quietly got up and left the table. His memory of this experience is that it was not only negative, but hurtful.

The second story is much different. A minister well-known in his denomination recently took his own life. In the face of the tragedy and mystery of such an event, the love for this man among those who knew him well was so apparent that one had only to read their comments to be moved deeply by their affection. In spite of the circumstances of his death, they spoke of his forever remaining a giant of a Christian leader in their eyes. The reason consistently given was his humble and gentle sprit. The various leadership positions he held could have tempted him into thinking of himself more highly than he should have, but clearly this was not the case. That is what will live on in the minds and hearts of his family and friends, that he was a leader who had the grace not to overestimate his own importance.

The real danger, of course, in overestimating our importance as ministers is the spiritual damage we do to ourselves. We begin to use other people for our own purposes. Their needs become less important than our advancement or our prestige. The demands of our ego replace the demands of the gospel. The minister who makes this mistake will eventually have nothing to say to people who are searching for meaning and purpose.

I once asked a woman how things were going with her new minister. In her beautiful, southern drawl she invented a new word when she answered, "Well, I don't like to say it, but I think he's kind of a 'braggott.'" I happened to know the minister and was not at all surprised by her comment. Within two years he had been asked to leave his position. He was too wrapped up in himself to help anyone else, or even to see others' needs. It was a bitter experience for him and the church. He left the ministry for a period of time, but reentered later. One can hope that he spent his time away assessing the reasons for his troubles.

The book of Job contains a lengthy section that speaks a stinging word to all of us in ministry when we are tempted to think more highly of ourselves than we ought, beginning with God's illusion-shattering question to Job, "Where were you when I laid the foundation of the earth?" (Job 38:4). It is a good reminder of where we stand in the scheme of things. What we do is important, as we shall discuss next, but the fate of the world doesn't hang in the balance because of it. Our successes and failures matter, but not so much as to give us reason to think we are indispensable to the future of God's kingdom on earth, or even to the congregation we serve.

The one sure thing about ministry is that ministers who are wrapped up in themselves have a hole inside they mistakenly believe can be filled from the outside in. Thus, their behavior continues to make it larger and larger as they drain the goodwill out of everyone around them. They cannot help but be unhappy and miserable. Only as they understand and accept that the hole is filled from the inside out do they have any chance for personal happiness or the experience of genuine joy that ministry can bring. Thankfully, most of us who get full of ourselves do not suffer from insatiable egoism, only moments when the lack of respect or appreciation gets the best of us. In such times ministry loses its appeal, but when we hold on, we recover sufficiently to see that while we are not all that important, what we do is, and that is what makes it worthwhile.

# (7)

# Don't Undervalue Your Influence

Once we know it's not about us, ministers are free to recognize and claim the pivotal leadership role we do, in fact, play in the life of the church. Nothing makes ministry more worthwhile or enjoyable than the realization that as clergy we play a vital role in the life of the church. Our position stands at the crossroads of every congregation's desires. We can facilitate things happening, and we can prevent them from ever seeing the light of day. Laity may not follow clergy leadership, but it is a rare situation where they can ignore it. If by nothing more than neglect, ministers can determine the fate of any idea.

The people who know this is the case are laity. They often have a better understanding of power than do many clergy. They look to us for direction, for guidance, for a sense of "captainship," so to speak, the sense that someone is in control precisely because they understand the crucial position we hold. Ministers, on the other hand, fear as they would the plague being seen as needing to control. Being a "control freak," as it is generally characterized, is the sin of sins among clergy. The label implies manipulation, underhandedness, seeking one's own advantage rather than being concerned about others. In today's climate, too many clergy interpret using power as being a "people user."

There are legitimate reasons for clerical power being viewed with caution. The current scandal in the Catholic Church because of pedophiliac priests serves as a tragic reminder that ministerial position can be used to terrible ends. The hands of Protestant clergy are not clean either, as more than a few of us have been guilty of sexual misconduct and abuse of power. But none of these examples of how bad clergy can be should lead to the erroneous conclusion that the use of power in ministry to good ends is a bad thing. Part of our calling is to get things done for the reign of God on earth. Waiting for that to happen without using the position we occupy to do all we can for this purpose is itself a vocational failure. As long as integrity is our guide, power is the engine for actions that make for good leadership.

What we are saying is quite simple: Ministers have influence. This is the power we possess. Laity, Catholic and Protestant, even in today's world continue to think of clergy as representatives of God. There is no more acceptance without question of what ministers say, but neither is what we say rejected out of hand without consideration for its merit. When a minister who plays golf is accused of having the advantage of a power not available to the other three members of the foursome, there is more than just having fun involved in the play. The gentle barb reflects an enduring conviction that clergy deal with "principalities and powers" not of this world and not normally available to ordinary people. Thus, "Father, forgive me, for I have sinned" is more than the words of a penitent believer. It is a statement about the way all clergy are seen by laity. We are God's chosen instruments. Laity may be used by God from time to time to do mighty deeds, but they still believe clergy are the primary emissaries of God on earth. That means we have influence.

The following story illustrates my point. On October 6, Jerry Falwell said on *60 Minutes* that the prophet Muhammed was a terrorist and that all Christians know that no peace will come to Jerusalem until Jesus returns to earth. A group of my colleagues and I decided enough was enough and wrote a lengthy article taking issue with the kind of Christianity Falwell and his brand of Christian Right believers represent.[1] To our surprise, the Minneapolis *Star Tribune* gave the article major play. It was then picked up by some Internet news services and carried around the world. We received responses from all around the country and from places as far away as Nepal and Norway. The overwhelming majority were extremely positive. The tone was more than simply one of agreement. The most common sentiment was gratitude for a group of clergy finally publicly taking issue with Falwell and the Christian Right. I confess to being surprised at the extent of the responses our statement elicited. Even the negative feedback confirmed what we are saying. Clergy still have influence.

This reality can be a burden to carry as expectations of clergy continue to be unrealistic, but it also opens up enormous possibilities for ministers who gain and deserve the trust of people to make a difference in their individual lives and in the collective life of a congregation. Influence is a sacred responsibility. Our words can help or hurt the spiritual growth and development of people. Our words can inspire or discourage them. Our leadership can point direction or create confusion in congregations. We do not hold a position of unfettered power, but clergy actually do wield significant influence in people's lives. An engineer decides to tithe to his church; a young nurse decides to resist lucrative job offers to work in a wellness center for the poor of her city; a college student decides to enter training for full-time ministry because of the example of his local pastor; and a doctor in Nepal finds encouragement in the words of clergy in a city thousands of miles from where he lives. Ministers are people of influence.

It is clergy who most often undervalue this fact. Ministry does not always seem effective to those of us doing it. We sometimes feel ignored, as if our words always fall on deaf ears. From our perspective our influence is minuscule. But we are wrong. We can and do make a difference in people's lives. There are many influences on people. Ours is not exclusive, but it is real. It is easy to overlook the monotony of the daily lives of the people whom we serve. They go to work in morning rush-hour traffic and make the same frustrating journey home in the evening. They have only enough time to eat a late dinner, often at a fast-food restaurant, and then get children and themselves to bed early enough to be able to get up the next morning and begin the same routine. At a point in midlife some of them begin to see that the values of the dominant culture are as impotent as we have said they were in offering any lasting meaning and purpose in life. It may be a mixed bag to describe this as an age of spiritual hunger, but there is a sense in many people that they need more in life than the next pay raise, a hard-earned promotion, or a romantic trip they've booked. At that point our influence can be life changing.

But influence means accepting personal responsibility for it. It is sobering to realize that someone may believe what we say or be discouraged by the poor example we set. This is not a call to be saintly, only that we show good judgment in our thoughts and deeds. Undervaluing one's influence is easy to do in the day-to-day work of ministry. But if overestimating our importance gets in the way of vocation, undervaluing our influence is tantamount to a false humility that serves neither God nor people. In fact, it becomes a burden to carry around. We are not the only voice heard in today's world, but we are one voice, and it is an important one that demands the very best stewardship of its impact. Ministry has enough detractors to make any minister feel ignored or invisible. We do not need to do this to ourselves. As long as people have spiritual needs, clergy will have a place in their lives. That we have that place is a singular privilege that should give even the most discouraged minister reason to believe in herself.

# (8)

# Don't Hesitate to Apologize

Many things contribute to strong personal relationships, but none more than saying "I'm sorry" when an apology is warranted. Every minister who has done marital counseling has in one way or another said this to couples in conflict. What every minister should know is that this wisdom also applies to the practice of ministry. Ministers are as apt as others to say or do something that hurts, offends, or upsets someone else.

One incident remains in my memory, though it happened many years ago. I was a seminary student serving a little church on the weekends. One of the members was caring for her adult son who was dying of cirrhosis of the liver. Though he was not a member himself, nor had he attended worship, I knew that I should go to visit him. But I didn't. Heavy schoolwork and less-than-stellar time management gave me superficial reasons for this neglect. Eventually he died, and despite my lack of pastoral care his mother asked me to do the funeral. A few days after the burial I visited this gentle woman of the church. She was not angry, though she had every right to be. What I most remember about the visit is that she shamed me without intending to do so by saying that before her son died she had been hoping that I would come to see him.

There were no words to offer that could make up for my neglect of this pastoral need. But I could say that I was sorry. And I did. It didn't relieve me of the guilt I felt for months afterwards. I have no idea if it made any difference to this woman. She showed no open hostility toward me and continued to attend worship as she always had. But the only real solace I had was the fact that I at least had enough sense to apologize rather than try to offer an excuse she would have been able to see right through.

I wish I could say that this incident was sufficient to prevent me from making the same mistake again, but that is not the case. Instead, having to apologize for words, actions, and inactions has become a staple in my ministry. Even then, I have not always been quick to do so. But I at least recognize that saying "I'm sorry" is a sensible and direct way to acknowledge to those with whom I serve that I recognize my own humanity in all its daily weaknesses. It also says something even more important—something I have actually learned from a politician in this area. In the last Minnesota gubernatorial race, the Independent Party candidate was a man named Tim Penny, a former Democrat who served six terms in the U.S. Congress. He lost his bid for governor, but he put his finger on the heart of all leadership when he answered a question about why he was running again by saying, "Leadership is about relationships, and campaigning is a chance to make those relationships stronger."

Leadership is about people, about relationships, about the give-and-take of human interaction. That is why apologizing for mistakes is such an important quality in ministry. Relationships of any and every kind need constant repair. Who better to set an example for attending to this need than ministers? Church members may not be as accepting of an apology as we wish they would be, but making the apology is what counts. It's a matter of doing what is right because it is right. How our actions are received is beyond our control. Saying "I'm sorry" when it needs to be said is the thing that matters.

I once read that an apology is saying the right thing after doing the wrong thing. All of us who serve in ministry at times do the wrong thing. Nothing ruins a day more than knowing you made a comment you wished you hadn't made or failed to do something you know you should have done. But failing to say or do the right thing afterwards only makes us feel worse. Yet how often time passes without our doing so. We get busy with another claim on our time. We are under pressure to finish the Sunday sermon. We have to attend a denominational meeting. The demands on us from so many people feel overwhelming. "So we are human," we say to ourselves. "We're not the first person to make a mistake," we tell ourselves.

The reasons for letting an incident slide are numerous, to be sure, and sometimes nothing much comes of it when we do. Except that we are the ones who suffer. Our spirits get heavy. The need to apologize stays in our mind in spite of every effort to push it out. The air between us and the person we hurt or argued with is thick. The strain is obvious, and its weight grows by the day. With enough time, though, the conflict becomes part of the past, but it is never quite out of sight because it is like the scar I have on the back of my thumb. I was putting up steel studs for a wall in our daughter's basement when my hands slipped and the sharp edge of the stud cut deep into the flesh. Later our doctor–son said it probably went to the bone. With butterfly bandages I managed to close the gash, and I continued to work. But two years later the scar remains because I didn't do what I needed to do to let the wound really heal.

The same thing happens in relationships. Ministers and church members have conflict because all of us are human. What ministers have to remember is that there are always at least three sides to every issue: mine, yours, and the right one. We may have been hurt or offended and feel that we have done nothing inappropriate or wrong, but conflicts are seldom that clean. And when the day ends, most of us know it. That is why the wound stays open. That is why our emotions are on edge. The incident runs over and over in our minds and will not let us go until we make an effort to reconcile differences or make amends.

The task that makes the failure to apologize so difficult for clergy is preaching. We stand before others and preach a gospel at whose center are themes of forgiveness, reconciliation, responding in love to offenses suffered, and the like. The stress of preaching— and indeed, the whole of ministry—when we are at odds with a church member and have not made the effort to resolve it, is enormous. We are fooling ourselves to think we can function this way without damaging our spirit. We may not succeed in erasing a barrier that exists between us and a church member, but apologizing is about making the effort so that we can feel good about ourselves even when we feel bad about what has happened.

# (9)

# Don't Be Afraid to Put Your Cards on the Table

It is a common practice, especially in large churches, for clergy not to be open about what they believe, how they read the Bible, or what agenda they have for the congregation. There is a history behind this approach. In previous generations certain powerful men (and it was always "men") would inform a new minister never to bring an agenda to the governing body of the church, but to allow them to present what he (and it was always a "he") wanted to do, and if they agreed with his plan, they would see that it got approved. These men believed this *modus operandi* was the best way to keep the senior minister out of controversy and conflict and the church running smoothly.

They were right, of course. As long as the minister and these power brokers saw eye to eye, the church ran smoothly, and the minister stayed out of trouble. But all clergy paid a high price in gradual erosion of trust and credibility. This way of functioning was doing ministry behind the scenes with a hidden agenda that created the perception that churches were run by "an inner circle of power." A church I once served had functioned this way during the days of its greatest numerical and financial strength. By the time I arrived, the congregation was in serious decline on both fronts, and the "inner circle of power" had been broken, yet a survey among the members revealed a ubiquitous perception that a small group of powerful people still controlled the church. That perception was a serious hindrance to the majority of the people taking responsibility for the church's direction and health and well-being. As I was often told by those who felt disenfranchised, "If the 'inner sanctum' doesn't approve, it doesn't really matter what the rest of us think."

Things have now changed in most churches, though not all, but ministers continue to be reluctant to put their cards on the table. Take for example, clergy silence in meetings in which issues of great importance are being discussed. These ministers work behind the scenes rather than being open about the direction in which they want the congregation to go. It sounds like an effective way to accomplish one's goals, but in reality it seldom works. In today's climate we hear much about "vision," or the lack thereof, in churches. Whatever one might think of the use of this term, it speaks to the need for strong leadership. The failure to be forthright in what one wants to accomplish in ministry will undercut this need. Clergy are the ones who must set the tone and direction for congregational life. With all due respect for the commitment and sincerity of laity, they simply don't know how to lead without a clergy leader. They are crucial to that direction being followed, and they can offer essential advice in refining it, but they are not the ones who set the signposts that indicate the way to go. That is the role of clergy.

The biblical example of this fact of life among the people of God is Moses. He was more than a man leading Hebrew slaves out of Egypt. He was the embodiment of God's called servant-leader whose responsibility it was to lead people to a land they did not know on a journey about which they grew more impatient by the day. The story of the exodus is one filled with the people wanting to go back to slavery, give up and die in the wilderness, or turn their affections to gods made of gold. Moses was the key to their staying on the journey and going in the direction God wanted them to go.

He is the model for clergy because the church is living in a modern day wilderness every bit as anxiety-producing as the one Moses faced, as well as offering temptations to idolatry at every turn. Timid leadership and the use of hidden agendas in meetings cannot equip people to do battle with the cultural gods working against the church's faithfulness to the gospel. Moreover, in this age of corporate scandal and distrust of leadership, even the hint of a hidden agenda by a leader will create a firestorm of anger and distrust that will undo any ministry. Moses spoke candidly to the people and candidly to God. It is the only way to do ministry with integrity.

One of the reasons so many clergy function this way is the mistaken notion that the "ministry of the laity" means the church must function as a democracy, yet the biblical message speaks of the community of God's people in a different way. "Theocracy" fits the biblical description of Israel and the church. Ultimately the issue is never what the minister or laity want to do. The question that matters is, What is the will of God? Discernment is not simple or easy, but it is the task churches face—that cannot be in dispute. Ministers are the ones to whom the responsibility falls for first articulating a perspective on God's will. Laity seek to affirm, refine, or change this perception of the divine will as they, too, work with discernment, but the minister is the initiator. Perhaps not exclusively, but the role of clergy is never diminished by the role of laity. Like Moses, ministers are leaders of a pilgrim people who are called to follow God, not their own will, and certainly not the dominant culture. Our work is to be open and candid with the people we lead.

Beyond one's agenda for ministry, ministers and laity are better served when clergy are also open about what they believe. Church members often have no clear sense of where their minister stands on matters of faith. This was a regular complaint of lay leaders in student churches when I was teaching. One might expect equivocation among student ministers, but it often carries over into full-time ministry. This hesitancy may be rooted in the fact that, in general, mainline clergy are more theologically liberal than church members, something that is a natural outgrowth of higher critical study of the Bible. But allowing this to make us cautious in being candid about what we believe is an unnecessary overreach. Every church has closed-minded believers who get upset and angry at ministers who in their view "don't believe the Bible," but placating these people with timidity about what we believe does not help.

One area that is in serious need of clergy forthrightness is how we read the Bible. There is an urgent need today for mainline clergy to share the fruits of their higher critical studies. Here again, fundamentalism continues to go unchallenged because we have failed to make a case against the way it uses, and misuses, the Bible. The irony is that such a case is easy to make. The simple fact that every translation is an interpretation and that every preacher is an interpreter of that interpretation is sufficient to show that fundamentalist claims of infallibility and inerrancy are bogus. But fearing negative reaction to how we read the Bible undermines any notion that we take it seriously. Lay people know when we are hesitant to preach in ways that reveal our approach to scripture, and they generally react far more negatively to that than they would if they knew where we stood and disagreed with it.

The challenge, of course, is having confidence in what we believe so that we can speak clearly and boldly about our convictions. In recent years mainline ministers have been put on the theological defensive as the Christian fundamentalist voice has grown stronger and more strident. But in this instance the best defense is a good offense. Ministers who speak with boldness about their own faith are likely to gain respect from church members whose own beliefs may differ significantly. Throughout his ministry, for example, William Sloan Coffin has been respected by friend and foe alike. Certainly his intellect and gift of speech are not given to many of us in ministry, but his openness in putting his cards on the table, whatever the issue, is an example that should encourage the most timid among us to emulate it.

A rule of thumb in ministry is that regardless of the face it wears, timidity works against effectiveness. Forthrightness is one of the small things in ministry that plays a major role in laity having confidence in ministers. This is not really about pushing an agenda. It is about being honest with the people we are leading. Timidity leads to game-playing that tears at the fabric of what it means to be in community with others. The minister who is not willing to stand firmly on what she believes or on what she believes a church should be doing will find it difficult to be effective.

Personalities naturally gravitate to certain styles of leadership, but whatever one's preferred way of leading, hidden agendas and soft-pedaling one's goals serve no useful purpose. The truth is that openness doesn't depend on personality. It is rooted in character and, therefore, knows no particular leadership style. One of my former students possesses a gentle spirit, but when one of his church members forced the issue of placing the American flag in the sanctuary, he stood his ground. He knew his view was a minority one and that taking this stand would probably lead to the man quitting the church. He was right on both counts, but today his leadership in this church is stronger than ever. Even more, he came away from the conflict more committed to his ministry there because he knew that he had spoken truthfully and honestly about his own faith. In the process a good ministry was made better.

Here's the deal. Staying in ministry is always in jeopardy whenever ministers' lack of inner strength causes them to hide their personal convictions when the issues are serious. Being open and honest when such leadership is called for not only strengthens the confidence of others in our leadership, it gives us reason to believe in ourselves. Without this, what others think will not make ministry worthwhile. With it, what others think cannot take it away.

# (10)

## Don't Idealize Motivation

A difficult task seminary professors constantly confront is shaking students loose from their idealism enough to prepare them for the realities they will face as ministers. One such reality is the degree to which motivation has been idealized when it comes to the service of God. We might say that while motivation is a good thing, what truly matters is making sure the interests of the gospel are served. This seems to me to have been the sentiment of the apostle Paul when he wrote:

> Some proclaim Christ from envy and rivalry, but others from goodwill. These proclaim Christ out of love, knowing that I have been put here for the defense of the gospel; the others proclaim Christ out of selfish ambition, not sincerely but intending to increase my suffering in my imprisonment. What does it matter? Just this, that Christ is proclaimed in every way, whether out of false motives or true; and in that I rejoice. (Phil. 1:15–18)

Paul was obviously facing a situation unlike anything that concerns us here, but the general point is the same. While any minister would wish that dedication to the Christian mission would be sufficient to motivate people to serve, the reality is that a lot of ministry would remain undone if that were the sole criteria for service.

This is not to say that motivation does not matter. When it comes to ministry it makes sense to think that why a person does what he does is important. What church wants a minister who is motivated by selfish reasons? What minister wants a church member to serve out of a need to be noticed or recognized? Common sense is enough to convince us that *why* someone does something can be as important as *what* they are doing. But the "why" does not usually matter nearly as much as we often suppose. Certainly ministers want church members to serve because they are committed Christians, and the laity want the same from their clergy. But it is easy for us to idealize motivation for service to an extent that becomes counterproductive.

The trouble with motivation is that it can sometimes elude us when we think we see it clearly. Most people have had the experience of doing something they later realized they did for the wrong reasons. We have also found ourselves judging the motivations of others incorrectly. More than once I thought someone genuinely wanted to do a task, only to discover that the person didn't. I have also had the opposite experience. The end to which they were working seemed to have little relationship to why they were doing it.

I speak from experience. We are a high-commitment congregation. Membership requires the signing of a covenant that defines the expectations our congregation has of its members. It also involves an annual renewal of this covenant. In this kind of environment I find myself making the mistake that this chapter is warning against. Once I preached a sermon about financial stewardship in which I said that if God doesn't have your heart, God doesn't want your money. It was a sermon about motivation as much as commitment. It was also saying that God is more interested in people than in their pocketbooks. As I think back now, though, the sermon might well have been heard as calling for a level of motivation few people can achieve. Commitment is what every church needs and every Christian should give. But human beings are not perfect, and the level of commitment and the reasons for doing something can be a very mixed bag.

Ministers know this as well as anyone. Some days we go to work because we have to, not because we want to. Sometimes we preach sermons that come from the head and not the heart. We make hospital visits we would rather not make. We attend meetings we wish we did not have to attend. We work with people with whom we would rather not work. There is much about ministry that would not get done if purity of motivation were a prerequisite. It is true for clergy, and it is true for laity.

This is not an argument for mediocrity. It is a statement of the human condition and the danger ministers face in expecting more than we should of people whose motivations are shaped and influenced by that condition. Becoming a Christian does not mean one stops being human. The counsel of Dietrich Bonhoeffer seems to me to speak wisely about idealizing church life:

> One who wants more than what Christ has established does not want Christian brotherhood. He is looking for some extraordinary social experience which he has not found elsewhere; he is bringing muddled and impure desires in Christian brotherhood. Just at this point Christian brotherhood is threatened most often at the very heart by the greatest danger of all, the danger of being poisoned at its root, the danger of confusing Christian brotherhood with some wishful idea of religious fellowship, of confounding the natural desire of the devout heart for community with the spiritual reality of Christian brotherhood.
>
> He who loves his dream of community more than the Christian community itself becomes the destroyer of the latter, even though his personal intentions may be ever so honest and earnest and sacrificial.[1]

Bonhoeffer wasn't making a case for superficial commitment in Christian community. He was simply pointing out the danger that ministers face of undermining the very thing we believe in by ignoring the reality of the human condition and by idealizing Christian community or dreaming of a church that doesn't exist.

The need, of course, is to strike a balance between the ideal and the real. This is an age of low commitment in every aspect of life. Conformity to this situation is hardly a way to build up the church. But unrealistic expectations only strengthen the impact of the dominant culture on church members. We who are ministers understand that important and effective service can be rendered when motivations are less than ideal and sometimes not at all pure. Our task is to speak the demands of the gospel without compromise, with an attitude that conveys an awareness of the real lives of the people to whom we are speaking. I see now that the sermon on financial stewardship mentioned above failed if it did not convey the word that while God wants our hearts, God wants our money, too, and tension between the two is unavoidable.

One of the primary reasons to resist the idealization of motivation is the matter of discouragement. Here again, I speak from experience. My moments of discouragement are in direct proportion to my expectations of church members. The more I expect, the greater my disappointment. Whether to have expectations or not is not the issue. Thinking they should be motivated by commitment to do more than they do is the issue. What helps me gain my balance is to ask myself how much I would do in Christian service or in the life of the church if I were not being paid to do it. No doubt a lot less than what I currently do, and that is the point. Ministers eat, drink, and sleep church life. Laity don't, although many of them think about it far more than ministers tend to give them credit for. But they also have other demands that have nothing to do with the church. It is understandable that they may be drained physically and emotionally by these demands to the point where they have little interest in serving the church. That so many of them do serve anyway is incredible. When I remember this, I am better able to balance the ideal and the real.

These days, it is common to see the words below on church signs:

## Ministers: The congregation
## Pastor: Jane Smith

In the abstract the sign tells the truth about the church. But in the concrete life of the church it expresses a hope more than a reality. That every church member would think of herself as a minister would be all the motivation needed for regular and faithful service. But the distance between the thought and the reality is one that few are able to bridge easily. In the meantime, a lot of ministry can be done. Moreover, we can trust that as it is being done, the Spirit of God is working to deepen commitment. Whatever the reason people do things in the church, the fact that they do opens them to experiencing the mystery of God in a way that heightens their desire to serve. Clergy know this is true because we have traveled this road ourselves. We can take courage that what God is doing with us, God is also doing with laity.

# (11)

## Don't Try to Leap Tall Buildings in a Single Bound

The sensible thing is not to try to leap tall buildings at all. David may have believed that with God's help he could leap over a wall (2 Sam. 22:30), but there's no mention of buildings. The wise path in ministry is to know your limitations and pay attention to them. Unfortunately, the superman or wonder woman complex is a temptation the moment one enters full-time ministry. This applies to physical limitations, but the real danger has more to do with the way we think than with what we do. One of the first and most difficult things young doctors have to learn to cope with is losing a patient. They work furiously to save them, but death sometimes still wins the battle. They will tell you that even though they know they did everything they could do, it still feels like a failure. They may have saved someone else, but the one who died is what they remember about that day.

Ministers have similar experiences. We lose people in various ways, and that is often what we remember about the day. And for many of us years of experience don't make it any easier. The other day I received the following e-mail from a man who had been attending worship for a year and then abruptly stopped. I had asked him to lunch to discuss his absence.

Dear Jan,

Thank you for the lunch invitation, but that will not be necessary.

> You are wondering why I am no longer attending SOJ. It's quite simple. This just isn't working. I am not a Christian, and after attending SOJ for over a year, I am no closer to being a Christian than I ever was. In fact, after the events of the last year (in addition to a lifetime of observation) I can only conclude that, at the very least, your God is on vacation.

My initial reaction was to spend the rest of the day running numerous conversations over in my head to see if I could have said something that might have made a difference in this man's experience or if I could have spent more time with him that would have helped him come to faith. And, of course, I felt that his letter was an indirect indictment of my failure as a preacher, resulting in yet another family being lost to a church that needed everyone it could get. A couple of days later I answered his letter, expressing surprise and sadness at his decision and making a request that he reconsider his decision to leave. He didn't, as you would expect. As I read over my letter, I see that it reflects a naive attempt on my part to get him to change his mind. It is a natural reaction, but what I initially missed, but clearly see now, is that his letter was in effect saying, "You didn't fix me, so I'm quitting." In retrospect, I think I would have felt better had my response told him that this is how I interpreted what he wrote, especially since this was the second time he had quit. Had I done so, I think I would have been able to let go of what happened more easily by not pretending I had the power to change it.

But ministers easily fall into the trap of being super "fixers." We try to be all things to all people, and when we fail, we think it is our fault. Further, church members like this man know how to work the situation to help us feel this way. They quit. They withhold their money. They create conflict. And they often win sympathy and support from other members who are just as troubled as they are. The hard truth is that in today's environment, more and more, the environment in congregations is becoming "toxic." A group of clergy in my own denomination recently sent a pastoral letter to all clergy and denominational leaders describing the situation in precisely this way:

> We believe that ministers and laity alike now "live and move and have our being" in a church climate of what

amounts to neglect and abuse and not, as we should, in the presence of a God who gives us life and breath and assurance and resurrection (see Acts 17:22ff.).

The ministerial vocation requires time, energy, and talent. As the environment of church life gradually turns poisonous in proportion to the systemic dysfunction that exists, ministers must use more and more of their energy and resources to keep up. Over time, ministers begin to wear down, and eventually exhaust their passion and vision for ministry. The wearing-down process takes an extensive toll. "Leaders of all kinds today are wounded, disheartened, disenchanted, and confused," says Bill Easum in *Journey into the Soul: The Loss of Spirit*. "Depression and fatigue seem to be constant companions in times of rapid change like ours."

The writers then draw the conclusion:

In conditions where lay leaders and ministers suffer injustices and unnecessary pain, presenting situations with a positive spin and hoping things will "pull up" sometime soon, simply adds neglect to neglect. We must not white-wash the outward appearance of our church while more and more lay leaders and ministers live and work in a corrosive environment.[1]

One may take issue with some of the statements in this letter, but it would not be difficult to reach consensus among clergy across denominational lines that congregational life is troubled. Owning and accepting limitations in this context are imperative. There are some people to whom we cannot minister, some people who don't receive a word from the Lord when we preach, some people who are unwilling to trust our leadership, and some people who will not respond to our overtures for reconciliation. The above letter cited one survey published last year by The Alban Institute in which 40 percent of congregational pastors said they have a serious conflict with a parishioner at least once a month.[2] This is an astounding statistic. It often takes clergy several days or weeks to recover from the emotional impact of even one conflict. For this kind of thing to happen with regularity can be devastating.

None of this says that the fault always lies with laity who have conflict with clergy, only that every minister confronts church members who do not respond positively to her leadership. Thank God, there are more who do, but the ones who do not can easily ruin a good day if we choose to let them. That choice will turn on how realistic we are about our limitations. Moreover, the level of our self-honesty will correspond to the quality of our inward life. Accepting the fact that others do not like us or think we are good leaders requires significant inward strength. Rather than working hard to serve everyone's needs, we would do better to focus energy on deepening our personal relationship with God. In the end, that is what will save us from being foolish enough to think we can leap tall buildings—or even a wall.

# (12)

# Don't Be a Stranger to Your Children

Clergy families are notoriously neglected. But when it comes to working parents, what child today doesn't experience feeling this way once in a while? Long hours and rushed schedules is the family norm these days. It doesn't help that ministers are not alone in this predicament, but it does mean that, in fact, we are not alone. This is why doing something about the problem is so important. Family is more than "family values." It is where we find our most important support or our worst disappointment. In short, family life is worth the time it takes to make it good. That ministers need to be told this is one of the great ironies of ministry.

There was a time in American life when spouses (usually wives) attended to the needs of family life for the purpose of freeing their husband-minister to do the work of the church. They often felt alone and neglected, but there was an abiding sense of serving a greater good by making this kind of sacrifice. Children were expected to fall in line. After all, childhood was a time for learning how to take responsibility for yourself as preparation for what lay ahead. Coddling the young was not an option well into the first half of the twentieth century.

But then life in America got easier. Free time for play increased, and the number of children being forced into the labor market decreased. Play was play. Then life changed again. Luxuries became commonplace. Teenagers went back to work, only this time for the sole purpose of buying the luxuries previous generations only dreamed of having, not to help put food on the family table. Today, the ease of contemporary life has given parents and children more opportunities to relax and play and do things they want to do, yet we feel hassled and rushed more than ever. Our days are filled more with demands than with fun. Instead of enjoying our children more, we experience the pressure of making sure they get carted back and forth to soccer and hockey and football and dance and karate and anything else one can imagine. Teenage driving has become the break from "cab service" for which most parents have been longing, adding one more vehicle in the driveway.

This is life as we know it today, and ministers are no less affected by what has happened than anyone else. We know what it feels like to have work and family time out of balance. Daily, there are factors within and beyond our control that play havoc with our schedules. In many instances family pays the price. I know few ministers who do not have more demands on them than they can meet. But the saving factor is that we are in a position to exercise more control over our daily schedules than many people can. Of course, people die without consulting our calendar, or go to the hospital, or end up in a family crisis of some sort. But on the whole, ministers can choose to take time for family and children. It is a matter of discipline more than schedule.

Consider this. A typical workday for a congregational pastor consists of three parts: morning, afternoon, and evening. Every minister has to think in these terms because evening meetings are an unavoidable part of church life. They are also the primary excuse for ministers' becoming strangers to their children. But only if good planning is ignored. It is an altogether good thing for ministers to choose to take the morning or afternoon for family when an evening meeting is on the schedule, or to plan some combination thereof. It is mostly a choice of disciplined planning. Let me cite two contrasting examples that make this point.

The first minister was divorced and had not remarried during the adolescent and teen years of his two sons. The fact that he lived in the same metropolitan area allowed him to see them on a regular basis, only he chose not to do so—not because he didn't want to, of course. It was always a matter of scheduling conflicts. A counseling session on an evening when one son was playing football. A church council meeting the night his other son was inducted in the National Honor Society. Never taking his boys on a father-son vacation because he just never took a vacation from the church. There was too much to do always. He failed to see how this was anything other than problems beyond his control. His sons didn't see it the same way, though. They felt as if they had an absentee father when they were growing up.

The second minister served as senior minister of a large congregation, but he made it clear when the church called him to the position that he planned to be present in the life of his middle-school-aged daughter. He never missed a cheerleading event, went on Saturday band trips, and was a proud father at his daughter's National Honor Society induction. He was sometimes criticized by congregational members when he missed a meeting they had planned without consulting his schedule ahead of time. Yet no one ever accused him of not working hard or of not putting in the hours such a large church required. He was a good manager of his time and was able to maintain a reasonable balance between family time and the work of the church.

In both these examples the highlights do not reflect the full scope of struggle each minister experiences in attending to family and church demands, but the stories do underscore something very important. The real issue we are talking about is emotional connection more than time management. The main difference between these two ministers is priorities, not poor planning. In general it comes down to this fact in almost all instances. Those of us in ministry are by nature needy people. We like being liked. We like to lead. We like to make things happen. We like being needed. Most people do. It becomes a problem when we need these needs met more than we desire to provide the emotional support to our families, which only we can give.

Being present to people we love is a daily choice for most people. Time does not work in our favor in this regard. We have time for family when we make time for family. One can be at home and still not be present. One can also be out of the home a lot and still be present. My own experiences as a child taught me this truth. My father left for Richmond, Virginia, on Mondays and returned home on Fridays every week of my growing-up years. As children we played on our local playground ball teams. Games were during weekday afternoons, and almost without exception, Dad would arrange his schedule so that he could make the two-hour drive from Richmond to Lynchburg to see us play, and then he would drive back for evening meetings. Those evening meetings didn't just happen to work out in his schedule. They were choices he made. When he died, many of the people with whom he worked remembered him for this kind of family commitment.

There were many legitimate reasons my father could have chosen not to be present to my brothers and me in this way. He made the choice he did because it mattered to him. His sons were a priority. There must have been times when he did not attend our games, but his presence was sufficiently frequent to make that presence my memory of him. Further, his being there spoke the language of love. My father was not a demonstrative man with his feelings, but his joy and delight in our lives told me all I needed to know about how much he loved me and my brothers.

That is what we are talking about in being a minister who is present to family. The most lasting contribution we can make to the world is to raise children whose values and priorities reflect the gospel we believe in. If we succeed in this, no pastoral failure will ultimately matter. If we fail in it, no pastoral success will ever be enough.

# Things to Do

- Be Prepared for Anything
- Show Gratitude to the People Who Love You
- Work Your Strengths, Not Your Job
- Use Your Ears as Well as Your Mouth

# (13)

# Be Prepared for Anything

Being caught off guard comes in many shapes and sizes because people come the same way. Former television personality Art Linkletter made a living out of children saying the "darndest things," but adults are not far behind. People of all ages say and do all kinds of things. It is one of the things that makes ministry fun. Every minister has a baptism story to tell or a children's sermon story that makes us smile. Once in a while we are recipients of a gesture that touches us in a very personal way. One year Joy and I received a gracious card from a couple who seemed anything but happy with our leadership. They said it was "minister appreciation" month, and they wanted us to know we were appreciated. On another occasion a woman sent a check to the church with the words that she believed in what we were doing and wanted to lend whatever modest support she could. Last year we went to our regional church board to ask for help in buying our first building. After an affirmative vote, a man approached us with a check for a thousand dollars, which he said was "to get us started."

Every minister needs to experience being caught off guard in these or similar ways. It can lift your spirit and keep you going in your lowest moments. Being prepared for anything doesn't necessarily mean that something bad is coming down the pike. Good things happen as well as the bad. But the negative is part of ministry, too. That people are unpredictable—all people, even the people the rest of us think are predictable, are unpredictable—means the best advice any minister can follow is to be prepared for anything.

For example, people quit the church for no reason. One of the couples mentioned earlier who left our congregation at a critical time lived a long distance from the church building and had begun to house hunt for something closer. Soon thereafter they invited us to dinner to tell us they had decided to move back to their hometown, which was in another state. Another time a woman we thought was sincerely invested in the life of our congregation dropped out with the explanation that she "needed space from God." A man who helped his congregation plan a capital campaign, twice making a pitch for people to pledge generously to it, walked away two weeks later and never looked back. I could go on, but you get the picture. All these people must have thought their decisions made sense to them. Ministers, on the other hand, are often caught off guard and sometimes never understand why people do what they do. But that is the way people are. They do what they do.

Ministers and churches seem to be especially vulnerable to the unpredictable ways of people and can often feel the effects for months or even years afterward. Perhaps one reason ministers are so vulnerable to this problem is that we have few ways to hold people accountable for their actions. Churches are not clubs with membership requirements that impinge on individual choice. Thus, members feel perfectly free to come and go, to give and not give, at their discretion. In our congregation we have taken steps mentioned previously to deal with this issue, but the reality we face at the end of the day is that people are unpredictable and we have no choice but to live with the choices they make.

The impact seems hardest on young ministers, partly because of the idealism with which all of us enter ministry. We trust that people are motivated by their love for God and their desire to do what is right in all situations. Experience may take these thoughts out of the best of ministers, but what we hope happens is that we understand that people who join the church do not change quickly, and sometimes not at all. Everything hinges on their willingness to do the work that growth entails. In either case change is slow. That it comes at all is worth celebrating, but there is never a point where being prepared for anything is not good advice.

So how does one do that? *By taking a small dose of cynicism.* Be cynical for a day, or for an hour or two. I am not suggesting that ministers become cynical people, as I will argue against later, only that we recognize that all people from time to time are motivated by selfishness. That is one of the definitions of a "cynic." Ministers, of all people, know this to be true. But somehow we've gotten the notion that we are supposed to pretend it isn't true, that Christians are supposed to look at life through rose-colored glasses. The opposite is more the case. Paul said it the way it really is when he made the case for salvation in Jesus Christ with the charge that "all have sinned and fallen short of the glory of God"(Rom. 3:23). A dose of cynicism is one way to wake ministers to this fact of life.

Being prepared for anything means we know that whatever heaven is, it is not church life. Congregations are cauldrons for words and actions exploding from the emotional baggage that people walk around with daily. Churches seem to be the one place they think they can "let it all out" without consequences. One of my former students had to break up a fistfight in a meeting of the church's governing board. This kind of behavior is, of course, inexcusable by any standard—and it happens infrequently, thank God—but it illustrates the environment of churches, in which anything and everything happens. Much of it will be good, and some of it will be bad. A little cynicism will go a long way in preparing us not to be caught off guard by the latter while allowing us to be surprised by the former. Better in that order than the reverse, if we are to keep our wits. What we are talking about is learning to expect that much will happen in ministry that is inexplicable and often quite hurtful. Both can drive ministers crazy because it is not easy to stop thinking about them. Things I don't understand become embedded in my mind. Hurts get into my heart. In its own way, each saps my desire to do ministry.

A mild dose of cynicism is another way of saying, "Ministers need a reality check from time to time to keep our feet under us." We cannot be prepared for everything that comes our way in ministry, but understanding the unpredictable ways of people will, by itself, be enough to keep our balance when the unexpected happens.

# (14)

## Show Gratitude to the People Who Love You

A friend has kept a gratitude journal for many years. Regularly she writes down things for which she is grateful: a conversation with someone, something she's read, or a special experience. It is obvious from her description of what she writes that she is very attentive to ordinary moments that could easily be overlooked or taken for granted—moments from her children, extended family, friends, church, her minister's sermon. She says keeping this journal has made her a more thankful person because it reminds her of the many ways her life is blessed. This is from a woman who has known many troubles: a child's divorce, a son with muscular dystrophy dying a tragic death because of a freak wheelchair accident, a husband of sixty years being told he had cancer and six months to live. That she keeps this gratitude journal is a marvelous testimony of faith.

Gratitude is something ministers tend to talk about more than they actually feel. In dealing with people of all shapes and sizes, the dose of cynicism recommended in the previous chapter has a way of becoming a predominant attitude. It is not easy to feel grateful when you're angry, upset, or discouraged. In her book *Attitudes of Gratitude,* M. J. Ryan says it is impossible, in fact, to feel grateful and have negative feelings at the same time:

> One of the incredible truths about gratitude is that it is impossible to feel both the positive emotion of thankfulness and a

negative emotion such as anger or fear at the same time. Gratitude births only positive feelings: love, compassion, joy, and hope. As we focus on what we are thankful for, fear, anger, and bitterness simply melt away, seemingly without effort.[1]

One would think that Christians, of all people, and clergy in particular, would already know this. After all, gratitude is surely one of the fruits of discipleship. To experience the truth that God is love, and that God loved us before we ever loved God, would seem to be more than sufficient grounds for Christians living life in gratitude. Somewhere I read a statement by Scottish theologian John Baillie to the effect that a true Christian was a person who never forgets what God has done in the person of Jesus Christ, and whose whole comportment and whole activity, therefore, have their root in the sentiment of gratitude.

Yet the reality is that giving thanks for life and ministry comes hard for many clergy who live with criticism as a daily experience. Moreover, we are in an age when surviving seems to be the goal of many churches, and moments of grace that bring strength can be infrequent.

At the same time few, if any, ministers do not have church members who love them dearly. These are the people who focus on us rather than on what we do. They greet us with a smile and eyes filled with love. They do small acts of kindness that let us know they are holding us close to their hearts. These people sustain ministers. The woman mentioned at the beginning of this chapter who keeps a gratitude journal is such a person. Having been her pastor at one point, I was the beneficiary of her loving support. She has always possessed the inward strength to tell me the truth when I needed to hear it, but it has always had the tone of seeking to build me up rather than tear me down. She loves "in spite of," not "because of." But as much of a treasure as she is, she is, in fact, not rare. Every minister has this kind of church member—more than one, in most cases. If as a minister names are not coming to mind as you read this, there is a good chance that you have fallen into self-destructive cynicism that is preventing you from recognizing the love that surrounds you.

But knowing we have these people in our churches is not enough. Ministers need to let them know we appreciate them. A telephone call or a written note is a small thing, but it means more than a little to those to whom it is expressed. Not the least, it lets them know their love is not lost on us. Recently I traveled to the city where a woman who has taken a special interest in our new church lives. My time there was short, but I decided to call her to say hello and to thank her for all the encouraging letters she sends to us. It was a small thing to do, but her response on the phone left no doubt that my call meant more to her than I could have anticipated. A few days later she wrote a letter that began, "I must respond to the phone call, so unexpected and so appreciated" (she underlined the last two words). Who would have thought that this simple expression of gratitude would mean so much? But why wouldn't it? Such expressions from her mean that much to Joy and me. Why would it be any different for her?

The truth is, ministers have more than a few people like this woman who are a constant source of encouragement. They show care and concern for us in numerous ways. We need to thank them, even if it is not something they expect or even desire. There is no such thing as too much gratitude, especially when saying thank you seems to come hard for many people today. For the people who love their minister, expressions of concern come naturally to them. If we never showed any gratitude for who they are, it would not stop them from doing what they do, but when we do say thank you, it lifts their spirits in the same way they lift ours.

Paul wrote to the Christians in Ephesus: "I have heard of your faith in the Lord Jesus and your love toward all the saints, and for this reason I do not cease to give thanks for you as I remember you in my prayers" (Eph. 1:15–16). This is part of a prayer in which Paul expresses gratitude to the Ephesian Christians for their faith and faithfulness. That alone is sufficient reason for clergy to be a thankful group. That people have faith and seek to be faithful is not insignificant. But Paul's is an excellent example of the general importance of periodically expressing gratitude to those for whom we serve as spiritual guides. We express gratitude because of their attentiveness to our personal needs.

But, of course, the people to whom ministers most need to show gratitude for loving support are family. These are the people who see the best and the worst about us and still love us. These are the people to whom we say harsh things and forget the special days in their lives. They are the people who will defend us to any critic and stand beside us in any trouble, even when they know we had a hand in what happened. Showing gratitude to family is one of the crucial elements of ministry. I know this not because I am good at it, but because I am not. I should be, though, as all of us in ministry should be, for who among us has not seen the positive effect that the smallest deed of gratitude produces in our own families? It should never be the case that any member of a clergy family would think that we who are known as "pastor" are concerned about others but don't seem to care much for our own family.

Gratitude. The root word in Greek is *charis,* or "grace." To be a "eucharistic" people means to be a grateful people. Gratitude, then, is born of a cross we did not bear, but which calls us to be its ambassadors in the world. That ministry starts at home and then moves out to all those who love us. As it does, it gains the strength it needs to be given away to those who do not love us and may even be unkind to us. That is when the witness of a thankful heart becomes truly winsome.

But as strange as it may sound, a grateful heart is a spiritual discipline that requires development. The fruits of the Spirit do not fall on us. They grow from tiny seeds and must be cultivated to come to full bloom. Like other attitudes, M. J. Ryan suggests that gratitude needs to become a "habit of the heart" for it to make a difference in our lives.[2] "Feeling grateful" is not the only way to be grateful. We can exercise mind power that allows us to think about reasons to be grateful when we don't feel that way. Ryan goes on to note that in the process we experience a great irony.

> The more you cultivate the attitude, even if you don't feel it, the more you experience the feeling. The more loving we are, the more love we feel. The more joy we radiate, the more comes back our way. And the more thankful we are, the more we experience the richness of spirit that grateful feelings produce.[3]

So gratitude goes to the heart of what it means to love God. And a grateful heart can confront the worst moments in ministry and keep on beating. It is a heart that will never give up or give in.

# (15)

# Work Your Strengths, Not Your Job

This is commonsensical advice, yet it is something that even the best of leaders overlook. One reason is that many do not actually know what they are good at. Their position calls for them to do many things, and that is what they do without regard for their true abilities. Ministers often get into this pattern, especially when it is a solo ministry situation with little or no support staff. The old phrase "jack-of-all-trades, master of none" describes the way many clergy function, which is bound to bring large amounts of frustration coupled with very little satisfaction. Why wouldn't anyone want to quit after a few years of this kind of ministry?

What makes working our strengths more difficult in ministry than one might expect is the fact that knowing them doesn't come from aptitude tests or career assessment, but from years of experience. We sometimes know what we like to do, but that is not always what we are good at. Part of discerning strengths is understanding that context is crucial. A strength in one situation does not automatically translate into a strength in a different context. For example, a marvelous organist and choir director who gives effective leadership in a liturgical worship setting made an attempt to play the keyboard for a contemporary worship service intended to attract young people. He played every praise song with the skill and style he brings to hymns. The result can be described as something akin to an orchestra trying to play country music. The musician's strength in one context was a weakness in another.

It is a fact of life that every minister needs to attend to if we are to enjoy the work we do. Context impacts how well we do everything in ministry. A minister I know is a good writer, but has yet to master writing newsletter articles. He tends to be lengthy and detailed in a context that requires substantive brevity. This is a task whose fruits are not proportionate to the labor involved. It is the way many ministers function.

Sometimes our strengths are expressed in tasks we do not like to do. A friend of past years was the best preacher I have ever heard. He possessed an amazing ability to balance inspiration with stinging challenge, and he did it with immense pastoral sensitivity. Once a church member remarked after worship, "I can't imagine a better sermon being preached anywhere in this country today." That's the kind of preacher this man was. Yet it was a burdensome labor for him. He never liked doing it and always felt inadequate for the task. But in the context of a small congregation that was known in the community for its witness to racial and social justice, this was one of his major strengths.

Context is everything and can be a helpful guide in discerning one's strengths in the midst of the many demands of congregational life. Tasks involving preaching, administration, hospital visitation, and counseling usually finish at the top of surveys church members turn in to search committees or judicatory officials when looking for a new minister. The list is much longer than these, of course, but these are the top choices almost all the time. Each is important, and each can take the better part of a week's work to do well, but of course, clergy seldom have that kind of time for any one of them precisely because they all clamor for attention. Context can be a key in discerning which of these is our strength.

Doing what we do well is crucial to spiritually surviving ministry. When it turns out to be something we truly enjoy, spiritual energy flows unhindered in all we do. A good rule of thumb to spiritual healthiness in ministry is to devote consistent attention to what brings us joy and satisfaction. We need to do tasks that make us feel effective and capable. Spending time on tasks that play to one's weaknesses without compensating by devoting time to those things that feed one's sense of purpose will kill anyone's spirit. The minister mentioned earlier who did not enjoy preaching, though he was good at it in the context of his ministry, had years before convinced the congregation to free him from preaching during the summer months to allow him to do what brought him enormous joy in ministry: directing a weekly day camp that brought together children from the inner city and the suburbs. He believed the camp was a tangible investment in the future, and it gave him more satisfaction than preaching could ever do.

Sadly, discerning strengths and weaknesses in specific contexts is not something ministers are educated to do. Rather, we are schooled to try to do everything well because most of us serve churches where we have to do almost everything. This makes choosing tasks much more difficult. The temptation to be the jack-of-all-trades and master of none seems to be a necessity rather than a choice for many ministers. But in truth, it makes having the discipline to spend time on what brings us joy and satisfaction all the more urgent. Years before I published a book, I spent time writing because it was (and is) the most satisfying part of ministry for me. At the time publishing was a distant hope, but the personal pleasure writing brings was still present. I learned quickly that pastoral visitation was important for building trust relationships with church members, but over the years it has remained a difficult task for me. There have been very few moments when I have left a hospital room, a nursing home, or a home visitation feeling good about what I said or did. I have learned to compensate for that sense of frustration and emptiness by writing. The style may be for a newsletter article, personal journal entry, scholarly journal, book, letter to a friend or colleague, sermon, or even a funeral meditation. In each instance the discipline of writing consistently brings me enough satisfaction to make any day in ministry worthwhile.

Yet embracing a strength we have is not easy for many ministers. I know I am a writer, but after years of doing it, I only recently truly affirmed this strength for myself. It happened because of the positive reaction to the Falwell article mentioned earlier. One response came from a man who is a writer himself in the form of a detailed letter, and later in person, in which he affirmed both the content and the writing quality of the article. I remember saying to myself as if someone else were talking, "Jan, you are a writer." But I suspect that most ministers experience the same struggle. We are quick to admit our weaknesses, but owning our strengths feels vain or self-serving, as if humility requires such denial. It doesn't. More than that, working our strengths means we first have to claim them. It is how we delight in them without becoming vain about them. To claim a strength is to free ourselves from the need for affirmation so that confidence in what we do well becomes reward enough. Working to your strength will give you security, a sense of inward balance that gives meaning to some of the things you do, which makes the rest of what you do doable.

Working our strengths is also a way of loving God. Jesus tells us to love God not only with our minds, hearts, and souls, but also with our "strength" (Mk. 12:30). Ministry is not about getting the job done. It is about showing our love for God. While we have no choice but to do many things we would rather not do and some things we are not good at, we can and must choose to engage in those areas of ministry that play to our strengths.

Once when interviewing for a faculty position I was asked what made me soar. I don't remember what I said, but I do know that I groped for words. The question caught me off guard. I had never been asked anything remotely close to it before or since, but it was, I believe, the best question I have ever been asked in an interview. I also believe clergy should be able to answer a similar one when it comes to ministry. Not every strength makes us soar, but one or two do, and these must be something we do on a regular basis, just for the joy of doing them. These strengths can and will prevent ministry from becoming just a job to do.

# (16)

# Use Your Ears as Well as Your Mouth

The old adage "God gave human beings two ears and one mouth for a reason" is more than a pithy aphorism. It is basic wisdom in ministry. Speaking and listening may be two sides of the same coin, but it's far from a toss-up. A listening ear makes for a more effective voice. It does not work in reverse. To have the reputation of not being a good listener makes ministry harder than it is, and every minister knows that ministry's degree of difficulty needs little augmentation. Most experienced ministers know the importance of listening because we have paid the price for doing too little of it. We can recall times when we should have spoken less and listened more, when we were too busy responding to pay attention to what someone else was saying.

But listening is larger than simply talking less. It involves paying attention to everything that is going on around you. A colleague was asked to resign his position in a meeting with lay leaders in which he thought he would be able to negotiate an increase in salary. He seemed genuinely shocked by their action. He may have chosen to ignore the signs of a deteriorating ministry, or he may not have seen it coming at all, but in either case he was guilty of not "listening" to his own ministry.

Sometimes the failure to listen can be so egregious that one wonders how a person, especially one in ministry, could be so blind to its effect. During my time at the seminary a new member of the faculty immediately got off to a bad start when during his first year he seemed determined to speak first and longest on nearly every topic on the agenda of faculty meetings. It did not take long for the rest of us to get the impression that he had no interest in understanding the lay of the land, so to speak, no interest in getting to know us beyond casual acquaintance, and he certainly held himself in such esteem that he thought the rest of us wanted to hear his thoughts before everyone else's. He was wrong, of course, and was terminated after his second year of teaching.

But the price of not listening does not have to reach this level of crisis to have a seriously negative impact on ministry. We've all run into people who have a better story to tell than ours. Many times they are likeable enough. They just never seem interested enough in what others are saying to listen. There is no experience you've had they haven't, no book you've read they haven't, no idea that came to you they haven't already thought about. The words of others serve as a springboard for the next point they want to make or story they want to tell.

Ministers can do better than this. Writer Patrick Henry tells the story of his former mother-in-law's repeating the table grace "Make us ever mindful of the needs of others," only she reversed the words and said, "Make us needful of the minds of others."[1] He says his first reaction was to think she had made a hilarious faux pas, but then he realized that what she had said may, in fact, have been inspired. "Make us needful of the minds of others" was for him a call to "shut up for a while and listen."[2] And well it should be. Such a marvelous twist óf words is easily remembered: "Make us needful of the minds of others."

In actuality, listening is not difficult to learn to do; it is a discipline anybody can learn. The good thing about listening too little and talking too much is that we can do more of the former and less of the latter simply by being conscious of the need "for the minds of others." Just yesterday in a church school class I experienced how true this is, and I witnessed the positive effect listening more and talking less can have for ministers. The topic was war and peace. I was asked to share a Christian perspective on the subject, so I chose to describe the "Just War" theories articulated by Augustine and Thomas Aquinas. At the time President George Bush had just announced two decisions of his administration. The first was a policy of preemptive strikes against any perceived threat to U.S. security. The second was an approval for the CIA to assassinate people on a designated terrorist list. Members of the class brought these two policies into the discussion, and within a matter of minutes things became heated. I sat and listened, making few comments. Time soon ran out, but the discussion continued among the class members for several minutes afterward.

Listening more than talking made it possible for me to think about what the various people in the class were really saying in their comments. I was surprised at the intensity of feelings some of them displayed as well as the perspective on the topics from a couple of them. Had I talked more than listened I probably would not have taken notice of any of this. Listening also gave me the freedom to clarify what was being said without supporting or refuting anything. I was able to "see" the right questions to ask. That is one of the benefits of listening: being able to ask questions.

I once heard Lou Holtz, head football coach at the University of South Carolina, say that he had never learned a thing talking, but that he had learned a lot by asking questions. That is good advice for ministers. Listening to the debate in the class allowed me to learn rather than try to teach. There is place for both. The trick is knowing which is needed when.

One of the simple truths about listening is that there is no credible reason for not doing more of it. Relative to speaking, it is an easy discipline to practice. Paying attention to myself so that I recognize when I am finishing another person's sentence or making sure I'm not being too anxious to make my point is not difficult. It is like any other discipline. It requires intentionality. Good listening may come naturally to some, perhaps to the introverted, but the rest of us have to monitor ourselves to do it. Yet it can be done without much effort. Making a covenant with ourselves to listen more and talk less is the place to start. It needs to be a goal of spiritual growth, beginning, of course, with listening to God. That is part of "obedience." Both Testaments speak of this human problem. The psalmist wrote of nations that worship idols, "They have ears, but they do not hear" (Ps. 135:17). Proverbs warns against closing one's ears to the cries of the poor (Prov. 21:13). The prophet Isaiah spoke of the hope of people's ears being opened to the word of the Lord (Isa. 32:3) while decrying the "deafness" of those who could hear if they only wanted to listen (Isa. 42:20). It is a theme running through the prophetic material. Jesus, of course, spoke in similar fashion, even quoting Isaiah's warnings (Mt. 13:14).

The point in these and numerous other passages is that the ability to listen is a sign of spiritual maturity. Thus, learning how to do it is a spiritual discipline. It requires attentiveness and practice. The more we listen, the more we listen. What is more, this is the kind of discipline that brings immediate reward. We leave a conversation knowing that we have demonstrated the kind of maturity we want church members to possess. In essence, then, listening is good therapy. As we have already said, good ministry and self-confidence are interrelated. Our weaknesses hang out for everyone to see, while our strengths often go unnoticed. But we can notice them, and when we do without becoming self-absorbed, it serves to confirm the rightness of our calling. Listening has that kind of power for ministers. Our work is to listen to the needs of others. As we do, we experience grace-filled moments that make what we do worth the sacrifices that go with it.

But that is not the whole story. As great as the need for ministers to learn how to listen is, we also need to be listened to. Every minister needs a confidant, a colleague, someone to whom we can pour out our soul and know that we will be heard without being judged. Many of us have weathered the struggles of ministry primarily because we have had such a person to turn to. Seldom do we find this kind of friendship and collegiality if we are not seeking it. Doors we don't knock on remain closed. But if we are watchful for a connection to develop between us and another, it will. The minister who does not have someone she knows will listen to her is taking a chance that the worst of ministry will get the best of her. In this regard, "Doctor, cure yourself" (Lk. 4:23) takes on a sense of urgency. Listen well in ministry? Absolutely. But also find someone who will listen to you. It may make it possible for you to be around to listen to someone else.

# Things to Know

- Know the Value of Another Day
- Know When to Hold Firm
- Know When to Fold
- Know the Difference between Pointing and Pushing
- Know How to Walk a Thin Line without Drawing One in the Sand

# (17)

# Know the Value of Another Day

You may remember the scene in the film *City Slickers* where Billy Crystal asks the rough-talking cowboy Curly, played by Jack Palance, "Kill anybody today, Curly?" to which he replies, "Day ain't over yet."

It's one of those classic lines everybody remembers. It may sound strange to say that ministers would do well to commit it to memory, but that is exactly what we need to do. The day is never over in ministry because at the very least there is always another day. Keeping this in mind when things become difficult or discouraging is what keeps us in ministry. Ending a conversation or an entire day feeling like it's all over, or you wish it were, can become a self-fulfilling prophecy if that feeling is not balanced by the perspective that the sun will, in fact, come up tomorrow, even when ministry looks its darkest.

The clergy friend who didn't like to preach but loved directing a summer day camp was an inspiring example of someone who knew the value of another day. In the 1960s, as the civil rights movement was gaining ground in Virginia, he and the camp's governing board made the decision to work on race relations by integrating the camp. They were able to recruit a handful of kids from the central city as a first step. The day after these kids attended, enrollment dropped from fifty to five, throwing the camp into a financial crisis overnight. But he chose to stay with the decision and to continue with the five campers.

Things didn't turn around quickly, but within a year enrollment slowly began to climb. Within a couple of years it reached the point of making it necessary to expand the camp sessions. Today, there is a waiting list.

There is always staying power in a situation in which a just cause is at stake, as in this situation, but knowing that "the day ain't over yet" works whatever the circumstances. I have certainly learned this truth in starting a new church. Many days have ended with the feeling that this ministry was over. We have gone through waves of people dropping out, moving away, or getting upset at our theological openness, and each time it has felt as if the end had come. But it didn't, and thus far it hasn't. It helps to remember this when times get tough. The end is always possible in a situation like this, but new life coming out of a crisis is just as possible, and knowing this is what gives us the staying power to continue.

Ten years ago a friend who is now in his twentieth year with his congregation went through what he says was the worst experience of his more than thirty years of ministry. A group in the church decided he needed to leave. They began an all-out effort to win support for their view. More than unkind, these people said and did things no church member should say or do and no church should tolerate. Throughout the ordeal my friend maintained his composure, itself a testimony to the quality of his character. He is also incredibly competent, and in the end that won the day. His critics realized they had failed and left. Ten years later the church is stronger than it was before because this minister knew the value of another day.

Another clergy friend knew the ministry she was in was not working soon after moving to it. Having just completed an effective thirteen-year ministry as an associate in a large church, the struggles she faced raised numerous questions about her capacity to serve in a senior position. It was tempting to retreat to the known and familiar position of an associate, and she had more than a few opportunities to do so. But she refused to give up even as she decided to leave her current position. Seven years later she is happy in a congregation where her leadership is affirmed and effective. She could have left ministry. She could have gone back to an associate position. But she chose to go forward because she knew the day wasn't over for her leading a church.

One reason knowing the value of another day is so important is that ministers bear the responsibility of setting an example for church members, whether we like it or not. Most of us don't, but that does not change the reality we face. Giving up is not a good example. The path of least resistance is quitting. Anyone who has spent more than a day in ministry knows what it feels like to want to "take this job and shove it." So have church members, which is why they need to know someone who does not let feelings determine actions. This doesn't require heroic sacrifices, but the stamina that comes from thinking through the consequences of one's actions before taking them. Early in my ministry a judicatory leader abruptly resigned over a conflict with a staff member. The judicatory board listened to the arguments for dismissing the staff member, but when they delayed action until they had interviewed this person, the official left the room only to return a short time later with a letter of resignation. One seldom knows the whole story looking from the outside in, but in my mind both then and now, this man set a poor example by failing to think before taking action, by letting his emotions make a decision that required more reflection.

It is admittedly easier to see it that way when it involves someone else, but there has never been a time when I wanted to quit (and I've felt this way more than once) that further thought about the ramifications of doing so didn't provide a better perspective on the situation. Most circumstances are less dreadful than they appear. We know this as parents trying to persuade a son not to quit college or a daughter not to rush into marriage. They survive when it feels as if they are throwing their lives away. Ministers who are on the brink of resigning a position or quitting ministry altogether need to hear the same advice from a friend or colleague. The hard part is that such counsel usually has to be sought, and that in itself takes forethought. But remembering that "the day ain't over yet" can prevent ministers from making premature decisions they live to regret.

Some would say that Jesus spoke to this issue when he said, "No one who puts a hand to the plow and looks back is fit for the kingdom of God" (Lk. 9:62), but this is more about discipleship in general than ministry in particular. Moreover, he seems to have said just the opposite when he told the disciples, "If anyone will not welcome you or listen to your words, shake off the dust from your feet as you leave that house or town" (Mt. 10:14), but clearly evangelism is the context for this statement rather than congregational ministry. But there is a parable that does offer some counsel on the value of knowing that there is another day, although this is not its theme.

The story is about two sons (Mt. 21:28–30). The father asked the first to work the vineyard, but he refused. Upon further reflection he changed his mind and did as his father had requested. The father, not knowing the first son had changed his mind, went to his other son and made the same request. This son responded that he would, but he failed to do so.

The context in Matthew's gospel for this parable is Jesus' conflict with temple leaders who are questioning who he is and the authority by which he speaks. Jesus criticizes them by saying that the people the priests consider excluded from God's mercy (prostitutes, tax collectors, etc.) will enter the kingdom before they do. While this parable does not speak directly to the subject of knowing the value of another day, it does suggest a few things that do.

The first is that follow-through is critical to intentions. The second brother failed in this regard. To make a commitment to ministry means doing it no matter what. There are no excuses for failing to follow through. A premature exit is such a failure. Ministries come to their end, but few of them require a sudden or quick termination by clergy. Congregations with non-appointment polity have been known to do this to a minister, but it is never justified and always rightly criticized. Clergy decisions deserve similar scrutiny. A bad day or a bad month may be nothing more than that. To make a decision to end one's ministry before the ending time has come is to be like the son who committed to a task and then failed to follow through.

Another thing this parable says about the value of another day is that first feelings are not always the best guide to a final decision. The first son refused to go but went anyway. How one feels at a given moment is hardly a basis for making ministry decisions. This son had the courage to change his mind. All clergy should keep this in mind. When things are difficult, it is tempting to spin everything around the cylinder of negative thinking, but the one sure thing is that this is not the whole story or a clear picture of the actual situation. Give yourself a break and admit that some of the parts may be blinding you to seeing the whole clearly. Instead of the ministry being hopeless, you may just be feeling the urge to run.

One last observation about this parable is that it points to the fact that what we do in ministry is by virtue of God's call. In other words, it's not "our call," even though we have to make the decision. That is an awkward position to be in, but it's what ministry involves. A salary package and family needs and the size of the city where the church is located not withstanding, ministry is not about what we feel or don't feel. It is about the call of God. Remember whom we said we work for? Sometimes we don't think about the value of another day because we don't want to. We want to do what we want to do. It's human nature to cast circumstances in a light that justifies what we have already decided to do or what down deep we want to do no matter what. But ministry asks more of us than that. This is about God, not just about us. Our will is secondary because we said it was when we entered ministry. Seeing the value of another day is a practical way to live out this high calling.

To go back to the parable, both brothers showed a measure of immaturity: the first one by his quick refusal to consider the father's need, the second by his failure to keep his word. In this respect, neither is an example to follow. Immature behavior never is. As clergy we can do better. We can refuse to give in to moments when discouragement hits and we want to give up, or worse, strike back. We can refuse to convince ourselves that it is time to leave when the truth is that our ego has been hurt. We can refuse to think that a day makes a ministry. There are good and bad choices in every situation. Ministries do in fact come to an end. But knowing the value of another day is a reliable way to make sure we know when that actually is.

# (18)

# Know When to Hold Firm

I am not a gambler, but I learned in my youth the wisdom of knowing when to hold and when to fold my cards. Poker was a favorite sport for Boy Scout campouts, though I don't think Nelsie Huffman, our scoutmaster, ever knew about it. We would sit in tents or barracks with flashlights in hand and play into the early hours of the morning. I was never good at five-card draw, which is also why more than once knowing when to hold and when to fold saved me from losing the few dollars I had.

"You gotta know when to fold 'em, know when to hold 'em." That's a line in the Kenny Rogers ballad "The Gambler." In the next two chapters we will be discussing both. Here, we can say that the minister who doesn't know when to hold firm is bound to lose battles that could be won and to give in on matters that could make a significant difference in feeling good about ministry.

There are issues worthy of fighting for. Fortunately there were role models who taught me this truth at a time when segregation was a way of life in my native Virginia. "Separate but equal" was the face of racism at the time, and seemingly a progressive point of view that more than a few clergy used to justify "going easy on the 'integration thing,'" as it was often called. But there were other voices courageous enough to insist that the church's soul was hanging in the balance when it came to civil rights. They stood firm and refused to play games with racial equality, naming "separate but equal" as but another way of continuing institutional racism. They marched; they preached; they participated in drugstore sit-ins; they wrote letters to the newspapers; they issued public attacks on segregation; and in the end they won the battle against segregation that no one believed was winnable. As a result they made the nation better and helped the church cling to a measure of integrity, all because they had the wisdom to know when to hold firm.

What they did took courage, of course, but first it took wisdom. Foolishness can be defined in several ways, but one of them is standing up for something that is not worthy of the sacrifice. Somewhere I read that philosopher William James once said that being wise involves knowing what to overlook. That's what makes it possible to stand firm on things worth standing on. The minister who fights for everything fights for nothing and is likely more interested in winning than in being wise. Jesus' parable of the wise and foolish builders (Mt. 7:24–27) can be heard as a warning about the kind of ground a person is willing to stand on when a storm is approaching. In ministry, causes can be great, and they can be trivial. Knowing the difference can determine whether or not we find ourselves on solid rock or in sinking sand.

But the challenge stretches beyond understanding what issues are important and which are not. How one goes about holding firm matters enormously. One of the ministers I admired during those difficult days of segregation didn't understand this fact of life. He chose to hammer away at the evils of segregation from the pulpit in an angry way. Church members who supported him found it difficult to defend his attitude. In the end he forced lay leaders to stand up with him or ask him to resign. They chose the latter, and a ministry that was making headway against this evil came to a premature and unnecessary end.

It is easy for people who are fighting for a just cause to ignore their own attitudes and methods that get in the way of people listening to them. Today I often find myself in partial agreement with conservatives on certain issues but unable to speak a word of support because their attitude makes me want to disassociate myself from them. One example concerns abortion. I find myself equivocating on a woman's right to choose without any restrictions at all, but when anti-abortionists call women who have had abortions murderers, I want to work against those restrictions

I believe are morally correct. Holding firm on important issues is not a license to speak and act without respecting those with whom one disagrees. Indeed, it is what makes effective leadership possible. No one who is made to feel like an enemy will listen to an alternative point of view.

Martin Luther King, Jr., was adamant about loving those against whom one was holding firm. Repeatedly he reminded his supporters that every enemy is still a neighbor and that in every person there are both good and evil, or as he put it, "There is some good in the worst of us and some evil in the best of us."[1] One of the fruits of this recognition is humility. Holding firm to one's position—fighting for what one believes in—requires a large measure of humility if one is to succeed. Pride gives birth to arrogance, and arrogance leads to more resistance rather than to dialogue. In all circumstances, and certainly in ministry, how one speaks and acts is as important as what one says and does.

One of the ways to remember to follow this simple advice is to remember the goal of holding firm. It is not to defeat but to win over those who oppose you. Here again Dr. King's words are helpful. He reminded his followers that their goal was not to defeat or humiliate racists. It was to win their friendship and understanding.

> At times we are able to humiliate our worst enemy. Inevitably, his weak moments come and we are able to thrust in his side the spear of defeat. But this we must not do. Every word and deed must contribute to an understanding with the enemy and release those reservoirs of goodwill which have been blocked by impenetrable walls of hate.[2]

Sometimes clergy do better at remembering this counsel when the issues are profound than when what is at stake is local and limited. I am part of a group that is working to change the organization pattern of mainline congregations. It is our conviction that current structures inhibit rather than enhance ministry, especially that of the laity. But resistance to changing structures, ineffective as they are, is usually strong, though generally a minority point of view. Those who resist want to exercise the tyranny of the minority as much as possible. Their interest is the status quo. Such people need to be opposed, which means ministers working for change in congregational life will have to hold firm against stiff opposition. But it has to be done in a way that generates support rather than attracting attention to one's own attitude.

In one situation a woman treasurer who opposed changes in the church's financial structuring arbitrarily paid the minister half his monthly salary. With pastoral skill but clear determination to continue implementing changes, he approached the governing body about the problem. Unequivocally they stood with him and instructed her to carry out their wishes. She chose to resign, and they chose to let her. The church today is much stronger than it would have been. This minister not only held firm to his convictions but knew how to do it in a way that garnered support rather than more opposition.

Amid the current conditions of church life today, holding firm is the only way to get anything done. Even if congregational life is not "toxic" in a ministry setting, the likelihood of unconditional support for changes in the way churches function is not strong. Anyone in leadership knows that mainline churches continue to be in trouble. Cosmetic changes will not do, because the real problems are deep and systemic. Ministers who are good leaders know this to be the case. They also know that once a direction has been set they will be greeted with subtle and not-so-subtle efforts by those opposed to force a change in course. Holding firm is not optional in today's church. It is essential because ministers carry the responsibility for direction. In an age of biblical illiteracy among those who attend church, how could it be any other way? Leaders are those who point direction, but in a church that direction is given, not created. The church is not a club whose members decide the purpose, mission, and standards for membership. The church is the body of Christ. Its purpose, mission, and standard of membership have been given.

This is why clergy leadership is different from most other professionals. Our task is to lead people into faithfulness, the standard of which is given in scripture. Ministers know that it is entirely possible to have all the cultural signs of outward success and yet fail miserably in the eyes of God. But many church members do not know. Their view of life is conditioned by a dominant culture that claims to know "the way to Oz," where everyone can find exactly what they want. Some lay people understand clearly that the American dream is not synonymous with Christian discipleship, but the majority, while sincere in wanting the best for their church, do not know what scripture says that would involve. Clergy realize this is the state of today's church. While we count it a blessing to serve with the people we serve with, we recognize that most of them have a limited understanding of the great commission, the extent to which they allow membership requirements to undercut genuine commitment, or the degree to which members who are involved are bogged down in institutional maintenance.

This is the reality of church life today, which means that change will come at the initiative of clergy because we are the ones who more than most are experiencing "cognitive dissonance," that mental stress born of the tension between what is and what can be. It's enough to discourage any minister. But what keeps us going is the battle for the soul of the church. This is worth fighting for. Thus, holding firm against great odds becomes the foundation for knowing that what we are doing is worthy of our full devotion. The risks are enormous, but the reward is knowing that we are being faithful to our deepest-held convictions about God's claim on our lives. That is what called us into ministry in the first place. It is what can keep us there.

# (19)

# Know When to Fold

Former President Lyndon Johnson once commented, "Politics is the art of the possible." To those who knew him, no modern American politician was better at getting things done than Johnson. Some of his tactics were strong-handed, but what enabled him to get legislation passed was his skill with "timing." He had an amazing ability to know when the time was right to move on an issue.

"Timing is everything" is a cardinal rule in leadership. Ministers beware! In fact, there is a lot clergy can learn from politicians when it comes to getting things done. They may not be held in high esteem, but effective politicians know how to accomplish their goals. Any profession that deals with people is political in nature. I once naively thought that churches did the right thing because it was right. Once in a while they do, but more often they do what an effective leader leads them into doing. And the one thing good leaders know is that "timing" is the critical factor.

The attention and response to the Jerry Falwell article mentioned earlier also brings this point home. When Falwell founded his "Moral Majority" in the late 1970s, a presumptuous name to say the least, I was the chaplain at a liberal arts, church-related college in Lynchburg, Virginia. On several occasions a few of my colleagues and I tried to call public attention to this development. We were ignored by the local and national papers.

Even when we were invited to address the subject in churches, people showed little interest. Two colleagues in particular spent countless hours taping the *Old Time Gospel Hour* television and radio broadcasts and then published a book of Falwell's own statements that left no doubt about his extremist views—but again, to no avail. In fact, the main attention they received was from area clergy criticizing them for devoting too much attention to the Moral Majority. Had the recent letter about Falwell and his Christian Right been written twenty-five years ago, it probably would have never even seen the light of day. The reason for the response it engendered today is "timing."

These public examples point to a fact of life about effective leadership. Timing affects everything, especially when it involves an effort to change the church. Those of us involved in trying to effect change in churches understand that the process for spiritual and structural transformation of congregational life works only in churches that are desperate for new life and, thus, are ready for change. This is why in most instances large churches resist it. They can be in a downward trend—or worse, they may have assimilated into the dominant culture completely—but they will continue to cling to the status quo as long as they have enough people and money to pay the bills. The seminal factor for those clergy and laity who embrace change is the decline their congregation is experiencing. If real estate is all about location, location, location, ministry is about timing, timing, timing!

This is true whether the issue is big or small, whether the change is significant or slight. One of the reasons is that groundwork is needed to get people on board with new ideas. A few people—and only a few in my experience—are always open to new ideas. Most of us are like a woman I know who says unashamedly that her first reaction to any change is, "I'm against it." Some of these people will never open themselves to new life, but many of them will if sufficient time is taken to educate them and prepare them emotionally to embrace the new. Many times this involves the kind of skill mentioned above that politicians use to get things done. People make politics necessary. People want to feel that the person proposing change takes them seriously, is interested in what they have to say, and then shows them how the proposal will benefit them. Would that clergy and church members together were concerned only with doing the will of God. But the reality is that traditions, personal preferences, a sense of security, perceptions of reality, and numerous other influences play a role in how people respond to new ideas and efforts to bring about change.

Knowing when to fold is all about timing. Sometimes the fight just may not be worth it, but it is more likely that it is a matter of waiting for a better time to get something done. The recent experience of a colleague is a marvelous example of what can be achieved when ministers pay attention to timing. She was called to the church where she is now the permanent pastor as a one-year interim. At the end of this time the congregation would vote on whether or not to call her on a permanent basis. Had she been a man, this would not have been necessary, but sadly this is the kind of discrimination women in ministry continue to face. But she was agreeable to the arrangement. This is a congregation that had once been the flagship church of its denomination but that for many years had been experiencing urban church decline. When she went there, attendance was hovering around sixty in a building that at one point in its life was home to more than a thousand wealthy members (when proofreading, my wife had a big laugh when she caught the fact that this sentence originally ended with the words "well-done" members—a Freudian slip?). The reason it has survived at all is the church's substantial endowment. During her first year the ministry stabilized as she helped those members who had stayed regain their sense of confidence and mission. Slowly she began to shift the members' attention from survival to ministering to the surrounding community.

At the end of that first year the future was a little brighter for the church, though many serious challenges remained. Yet when the congregational meeting was held to determine her future, as well as that of the church, things could not have gone worse. Staff members who felt threatened by her leadership joined together in opposition to her continued leadership, recruiting people who had not attended for years to be present to cast a vote against her. It was an ugly scene. Harsh words between members were exchanged. Two people actually began to shove each other. Order was restored, and it was finally decided that the vote should be postponed until a judicatory leader could be brought in to arbitrate the situation. The pastor could have quit, and no one would have blamed her. Some of her supporters, in fact, thought that would be the best thing for her personal welfare. But she chose to back away from pressing for a vote, and if the congregation agreed, she would continue as interim for another year, which they did agree to in a meeting two weeks later.

Her second year built on the first as the congregation launched a ministry to feed people in the neighborhood, which now has grown to the point that more than a thousand people each month benefit from this outreach. In addition other churches now contribute financial support, and still others send members who offer personal assistance in serving the meals. This outreach ministry will eventually lead to further assistance to these individuals and families as ways to help them become self-reliant are developed. In addition, a ministry to community children has begun that brings them to the church for education, recreation, and affirmation. These and other missions have given the members a new sense of direction and meaning. They are beginning to see that they once again have a reason to exist. It was not a surprise that in the congregational meeting a year after the horrible events of the first year they named this woman as their permanent pastor without rancor or opposition.

This powerful, even inspiring, story is an instructive example of the value of knowing when to fold rather than to quit or to hold firm. Quitting was the easy option for this pastor, and holding firm was the great temptation. She was wise enough to see that neither offered a way for the ministry to continue. The inner strength she showed in resisting both speaks of that which makes folding without losing face or confidence possible. So often ministers quit or hold firm because of anger or pride. This woman had the depth of spirit and commitment to read the circumstances accurately and to fold temporarily in order to achieve the long-term goal. Today the staff members who acted unethically are gone. Today the spirit of the congregation is positive rather than combative. Today the church is witnessing to the gospel rather than denying it in its attitudes and behaviors. Today the members are focused on how to reach out rather than on how to hang on.

All of it is a testimony to knowing how lose a battle in order to win the war.

Folding does not end this way in every instance. To use it as a means to achieve a goal requires spiritual maturity and confidence in one's own leadership. One without the other will lead to quitting or holding when folding would be better. In balance they form an inward strength that makes a positive impression on others. Folding can and will be viewed as weakness unless it is guided by this kind of leadership, a leadership that most ministers can provide if they truly desire to discern the time for holding and the time for folding. Taking the time to weigh the options and taking the long view of one's ministry make it possible. This woman certainly has leadership gifts not every minister possesses, but her example is not so unique that it cannot be emulated. Of all the qualities required in knowing when to fold and then having the ability to do so, spiritual strength is the most important. It is available to all ministers. Indeed, the minister who lacks spiritual depth will likely never know when to fold, and should he know that, he will not possess the inner strength to do it with grace and confidence.

Folding when the timing is right for it also allows clergy to do something most find very difficult: ask for help. The day after the fiasco in the above example the pastor called her judicatory official and asked for help. He was present at the next meeting. Jealousy and professional standing make too many ministers reluctant to ask for advice and guidance from colleagues. But if we have the courage to step back from circumstances that cannot be pushed, asking for help is a natural second step. And it is one that may hold the key to the future of our ministry.

What we are saying is that folding is a means to an end, not an end in itself. Giving up the struggle at one point can be a step toward success at a later time. Stepping back in ministry is a leadership strategy when ministers understand the power of timing and have the inward strength to pay attention to it. This is also how ministers keep their spirits up and their commitment firm. It can be seriously demoralizing to have to back off at a crucial point if it is not seen as part of the way to achieve the overall goal. It's the long haul that matters in ministry. As long as holding firm and folding are alternating sides of the same strategy to achieve our desired goals, either and both will provide a sense of being faithful to one's call. As the wisdom writer put it, "For everything there is a season, and a time for every matter under heaven...a time to keep silence, and a time to speak" (Eccl. 3:1, 7b).

# (20)

## Know the Difference between Pointing and Pushing

"Leaders point direction better than most." So says Robert Greenleaf, Quaker philosopher and paid thinker for AT&T for more than thirty-five years.[1] It is the most insightful description of the role of ministers I know. We are called to be "pointers," people who know the path to follow. But to be able to point direction, you have to know where you're going. The good thing is that clergy don't have to determine the direction. It is given to us. Our responsibility is to know it and then point the way to it. This doesn't come from reading books like this. It doesn't come from studying what other churches are doing and duplicating it. It involves a thorough and ongoing immersion in scripture and in history. These two areas can provide us the information we need to discern where the church needs to go (and not go), what it needs to do, and how it can achieve both.

Discerning direction for the church means our destination is not up to us. We are like couriers who have a gift and an address and must find the best route to take us there. The church's mission is a divine one. It's not up to us to decide what to do. It's up to us to figure out how to do what we have been told to do. Going into the world with the message of Jesus is not one option among many. It is the only option the church has. Pointing direction is the means by which we lead congregations to do the mission they have been given. This responsibility places enormous pressure on pastors to build up passion among our people for this great mission. While the ways of making Jesus known are many, there is but one ingredient needed to do it: will. Churches need people with the will to be missionaries, ambassadors, witnesses, servants— in short, church members faithful to their calling. Some possess this will. More don't. This is when frustrations can quickly build in clergy. The mission is so clear to us. The need is great, and in numerous ways we point the direction to follow, but our efforts are met with little enthusiasm. We cannot seem to get people to do anything beyond the minimal. It is precisely at this moment that the shift from pointing to pushing is usually made. We don't want to point; we want to yell. We want to get in somebody's face, to scream as loud as we can, "I'm mad as hell, and I'm not gonna take it anymore!"

Well, that may be a bit of an exaggeration, but the gist of it is true. We who are the representatives of Christ on earth depend on the will of people over whom we have no real power and sometimes no significant influence to fulfill our own vocation. It is a situation ready-made for high blood pressure. To suggest that pointing rather than pushing will ease this tension would be absurd on its face, but knowing that doesn't change the fact that pointing rather than pushing will ease this tension. Here's why. Pointing reflects an acceptance of the nature of ministerial leadership, which is persuasive, not coercive, and not even authoritative. If there was any genuine clergy authority in mainline church life, it dissipated a long time ago. This is the age of "no authority but my own." Modernity's mantra is, "I do what I do when I want to do it," and living in a postmodern world hasn't changed it in the least. The only chance ministers have of sleeping at night is to adopt the strategy of pointing.

This is not giving up or giving in. It is, rather, trusting that pointing is not as impotent as it may seem. Many years ago Quaker scholar Elton Trueblood suggested that the metaphor of "player-coach" was an appropriate way to describe the role of ministers in the life of the church. A rigorous thinker who offered numerous practical suggestions for confronting the problems the church was facing before anyone else even understood what was happening, Trueblood believed this metaphor captured the essence of what an "equipping ministry" of which the apostle Paul spoke (Eph. 4:11–12), might entail. He said a "player-coach" is a discoverer, what scripture refers to as an evoker of gifts, one who develops and trains players to use their own talents and abilities to do what they are in a position to do. In addition, he wrote, a "player-coach" is called to be an "encourager" of others, to help them believe in themselves even as they depend on others for help. He believed pastors could be "player-coaches" for laity, encouraging and teaching them to become the dynamic force for the gospel they could be. He acknowledged that sometimes the effort would require more time and energy than would be the case if clergy did it themselves, but in the end the reward would be in the multiplication of workers in the fields.[2]

But—and here is the key—equipping is possible only when the goal is clear. Players don't play the game to play the game. They play to win. Similarly, church members don't serve to serve. They serve to achieve a greater end. Ministers have to point out what this is. We have to articulate the end to which we are working in a way that is sufficiently compelling to make them want to share in getting there. That is what a pointer does. Pushing people to come along doesn't get them on board. Pointing to a mountaintop they can see might. Trueblood provided a winsome statement of the power of pointing when he wrote:

> Fundamentally, [the player-coach] is called to be a catalytic agent, often making a radical difference while being relatively inconspicuous. This is a high ideal. Indeed, it is an ideal so high that it can be made attractive to the very [people] who are repelled by the lower ideal which is the only one which some of them have hitherto known. Such an ideal, if genuinely accepted, can provide a practical starting point for reconstruction of the Church. It is not the end of the matter, but is undoubtedly a viable beginning.[3]

The literal definition of *catalyst* is "anything that precipitates a process or an event without being consumed in the process." This is the challenge of ministry: to do what we do without being consumed by it. Knowing the difference between pointing and pushing is how we can keep this balance. Pushing causes ministers to lose sight of the limitations inherent in the position we occupy. Moreover, it always creates resistance, and even when we get a few to join the journey, it often requires us to keep priming the pump, so to speak, to keep things flowing. It's what is called "high-maintenance" ministry. This sort of thing can eventually drain the life out of any leader. Pointing is a practical way to avoid "high-maintenance" situations. It is positive and assertive but stops short of assuming responsibility for the response of others. Just as no one can make another person into a Christian, so clergy cannot make church members into servants. That is something they have to want to be first.

Furthermore, even when pointing seems to be getting few results, it continues to be an effective way for ministers to avoid being weighed down by the demands of institutional maintenance. Ministers are not office managers or budget directors or executive officers. We are the representatives of Christ called to equip others for the work we do by calling out their gifts and teaching them how to develop their talents. Our role is to help them see themselves the way God sees them and to be willing to risk reaching beyond the "known" to make an effective witness. It's a matter of tone as much as anything. Because pushing creates resistance, which in turn causes frustration, our tone can become harsh and our heart, heavy. We end up not liking ourselves or the people we are serving. This is when ministry loses its joy. Pointing doesn't save one's ministry, but it is a way to step back from this abyss to see the road ahead more clearly. Once we do, our desire to share what we see with our people is rekindled. It is then that our passion for the gospel becomes contagious. We have balance again and are ready to lead with a clear sense of direction and confident spirit. Above all, we will be doing ministry aware of our limitations without being discouraged by them.

# (21)

# Know How to Walk a Thin Line
# without Drawing One in the Sand

The subject of this chapter builds on what we said in the previous one. To draw once again from the insights of Elton Trueblood, he also suggested that in order for ministers to prepare church members for ministry, congregations would need to be "reconstructed into the pattern of a small theological seminary with the pastor as the professor."[1] The primary subject, he went on to say, would be theology—that is, the knowledge of God.

It is an idea whose time has still not come, but it is one that would revolutionize the church if it were taken seriously. With few exceptions, seminary is one of the rich experiences in a minister's life. Though its inadequacies and limitations are well documented, theological study remains one of the great educational experiences a person can have. A concentrated time for the exchange and debate of issues that truly matter—the ways and will of God, the person and ministry of Jesus, the theology of both Testaments, the nature of the church and the respective roles of clergy and laity— all of it is a life-changing and life-shaping experience.

Trueblood's point, though, is that this kind of education should not be for clergy only. Laity also need and deserve the opportunity to discuss and debate matters of faith and practice. But if it is going to happen— indeed, if any in-depth study is to play a role in the equipping of laity—as clergy we will have to find a way to help them believe that we know how to walk a thin line of disagreement without drawing one in the sand. In short, there is a need for ministers to teach laity that we can disagree with one another without falling into disharmony. If we don't, ministry will be an endless fire alarm calling us to put out yet another flame before the situation gets out of control. I know of nothing that causes ministers to lose their zeal more than this.

One of the first surprises of my ministry was discovering the degree to which laity believe disagreeing with the minister inevitably creates a breach in the relationship. At the time I was in seminary and spent weekdays engaged in constant debate with students and faculty. Making a vigorous defense of my beliefs became a way of life. It was a shock to find out that church members with whom I disagreed on a host of issues, especially segregation, believed that I didn't like them as people.

It is not an uncommon experience in all relationships. People do not know how to disagree without being disagreeable, especially today when on a national level it is common for politicians to demonize their opponents. The unique dimension in the clergy–laity relationship is the tendency of a layperson to project onto the minister his own inability to disagree respectfully. Certainly ministers do the same thing, but if for no other reason than job security, most ministers are loath to get into verbal disagreement, albeit civil, with church members. Laity are not quick to distinguish between clergy passion and clergy anger. For this reason ministers tend to disengage from a rigorous debate with a layperson as quickly as possible. While it may seem to be the better part of valor, in truth, it testifies to the failure of clergy and laity to be real with one another and for each to act as Christians when they disagree.

Once I preached a series of sermons on controversial issues facing the church, such as abortion, homosexuality, capital punishment, prayer in public schools, and others during the time I was writing the book *How to Be an Open-Minded Christian without Losing Your Faith.*[2] I did so because I believed I should raise these matters where I served before encouraging colleagues to follow suit. Discussion groups were formed as well to allow church members to discuss the sermons. A Thursday-morning breakfast group already in existence swelled from three people to twelve. One young couple in their twenties who attended thought my call to open-mindedness on homosexuality was a rejection of scripture. I think all who were present would agree that I went out of my way to affirm their freedom to believe what they believed, but I also invited them to listen to the other side of the issue as well. Further, I was clear with them that in our congregation, disagreement was not a justification for personal judgmentalism, and that our hope and intention as a new church was to become a community of believers who could love one another in disagreement. They could not hear this invitation. Shortly thereafter they chose to leave the church.

This experience illustrates why ministers find it difficult to trust laity's ability to accept open debate and honest disagreement as the rules of theological engagement. I personally know ministers who do little in the way of Bible teaching of any kind for this same reason. Their experience is that differing points of view on issues cause division rather than debate, so they avoid them. But doing so negatively affects ministers and churches. The gospel must connect with life this side of death to have earthly value. No minister can thrive when the tough issues of life are off-limits in the church. It has all the feel of irrelevancy. It also suggests that church life is too fragile to be taken seriously.

The alternative is to be willing to run the risk of losing people who do not know how to be in a community of diverse points of view on controversial issues. But for a congregation to be such a community, clergy have to model behavior that demonstrates loving those with whom one disagrees. Refusing to engage serious issues with laity is no answer to potential tension. It is to follow such moments with pastoral care that conveys a consistent message of reconciliation, that witnesses to our capacity to show that we know how to walk a thin line without drawing one in the sand.

What this means is that the responsibility for setting the tone of discussion lies with clergy. Great issues confront churches. One of the weaknesses of the church's witness is the general perception that ministers and laity cannot disagree without causing a split. Ministers must lead the way in changing this image by addressing issues with pastoral care and pastoral sensitivity. This can be done when the minister's view is stated in a way that intentionally invites discussion rather than stating conclusions in a manner that stifles it. The good thing is that this approach fits mainline church life that has always affirmed freedom of thought even when we have not practiced it. The role of mainline clergy depends less on authority and more on authenticity. Knowing how to walk a thin line without drawing one in the sand is an opportunity to demonstrate what this means in the clergy-laity relationship.

Such an example also gives energy to ministers. Nothing substitutes for the feeling that we are helping people confront the great issues of life from a Christian perspective. Nor is anything more important. To know that this is how we spend our days cannot help but invigorate one's ministry and provide the patience and strength to carry out the less-satisfying responsibilities that go with ministry. Playing it safe is deadly for churches and clergy alike. Walking a thin line may take every ounce of will and control we possess, but when it is done effectively, we go to bed at night knowing that we have made a witness to the gospel the Holy Spirit can use to change someone's life. It doesn't get any better than that.

# What to Do When You Want to Quit Anyway

■ Go Back to Things to Remember

# (22)

# Go Back to Things to Remember

If you have actually read this entire book instead of skipping around, and you find yourself still thinking about leaving ministry or buying Powerball tickets to be able to take early retirement, then a second read will probably do you little good. But all is not lost. There is one last thing you can do. Give yourself a break by taking a break. Read some books or take in a few movies. Below are some suggestions with comments. For a day or two put away your theology books. Quit thinking about church and ministry. On my worst days a nonreligious book or a good movie does wonders to strengthen my resolve to stay in ministry, and even to enjoy it, when I might otherwise throw in the towel. I am not sure why it works this way, except that sometimes they help me to get lost in another world or to think about something other than discouragement. Sometimes life outside the church helps me to continue my life in the church.

This list may or may not help you. That is for you to decide. But my hope is that in moments when you are wondering if being a minister is worth it after all, one of these suggestions might contribute to your deciding the answer is yes. At least they might give you a break from the tension ministry brings and encourage you once again to seek out the resources you have already found that keep you going.

## — Novels —

*Pilgrim at Tinker Creek* by Annie Dillard
(To get away from it all by getting lost in a book exquisitely written)

*Watership Down* by Richard Adams
(An incredible story of rabbits and the human race)

*The Poisonwood Bible* by Barbara Kingsolver
(A novel about a missionary family from—we can be glad—a past generation)

*Prodigal Summer* by Barbara Kingsolver
(A marvelous book by one of today's best writers)

*The Thorn Birds* by Colleen McCullough
(For when you experience your own feet of clay and need to know you still have a place in ministry)

*WLT* by Garrison Keillor
(To make you laugh)

*Me by Jimmy (Big Boy) Valente* by Garrison Keillor
(To make you laugh again)

*A Prayer for Owen Meany* by John Irving
(To make you laugh and cry)

*The Cider House Rules* by John Irving
(A controversial portrait of abortion before *Roe v. Wade*)

*A Widow for One Year* by John Irving
(Just to experience the power of a great writer)

*The Mitford Series* by Jan Koran
(Novels actually worth reading focused around the life of a clergyman)

*The Horse Whisperer* by Nicholas Evans
(Worthy of its best-seller status)

*The Loop* by Nicholas Evans
(A good follow-up to its best-selling predecessor)

*The Notebook* by Nicholas Sparks
(A glimpse into life—and love—in the twilight years—perhaps the only book by this author worth reading)

*Night* by Elie Wiesel
(Wiesel finally speaks of the unspeakable.)

*Dawn* by Elie Wiesel
(A necessary word of hope after *Night*)

*The Town Beyond the Wall* by Elie Wiesel
(The story of a young Jewish man's journey to life)

*A Beggar in Jerusalem* by Elie Wiesel
(Wiesel's best work, in my humble opinion)

*The Oath* by Elie Wiesel
(On the necessity of being free to speak truth)

# — Nonfiction —

*The Death of Common Sense* by Philip Howard
(To understand why people do dumb things)

*A Civil Action* by Jonathan Harr
(To see just how corrupt corporate America can be)

*I Know Why the Caged Bird Sings* by Maya Angelou
(A moving story of the author's life as an African American girl growing up in America)

*Tuesdays with Morrie* by Mitch Albom
(A book that can change your life)

*Messengers of God* by Elie Wiesel
(Biblical stories told from the provocative perspective of a survivor)

*Lenten Lands: My Childhood with Joy Davidman and C. S. Lewis* by Douglas H. Gresham
(A love story worth reading)

*Out of My Later Years* by Albert Einstein
(Reflections on important issues by a brilliant mind)

*High Tide in Tucson* by Barbara Kingsolver
(The best book of essays I have ever read)

*The Long Gray Line* by Rick Atkinson
(Vietnam made personal through the story of the 1966 class of West Point)

*Buck Up, Suck Up, and Come Back When You Foul Up* by James Carville & Paul Begala
(An irreverent book that will make you laugh and help you be a better leader)

*The Road Less Traveled* by Scott Peck
(Especially for when you're falling into self-pity and need a swift kick in the—)

## — Films —

*My First Mister*
(A moving portrait of relationships seen through the eyes of a teenager, with Leelee Sobieski and Albert Brooks)

*Damaged Care*
(The true story of Dr. Linda Peeno's fight with the managed health system in this country—produced by Laura Dern, who plays the leading role)

*The Prince of Tides* (and the novel by Pat Conroy)
(A story of life in a post–dysfunctional childhood world—Nick Nolte in one of his best roles, and Barbra Streisand's not bad either)

*We Were Soldiers*
(Based on the events of the first U.S. engagement with the North Vietnamese—Mel Gibson in a film worthy of his talent)

*Cool Hand Luke*
(The film for which Paul Newman should have won an Academy Award)

*The Shawshank Redemption*
(A raw portrayal of injustice, corruption, and perhaps some redemption—Morgan Freeman and Tim Robbins form an amazing duo)

*Dead Man Walking*
(Based on a true story written by Sister Helen Prejean—Susan Sarandon and Sean Penn give unforgettable performances)

*Philadelphia*
(A film about the misunderstanding and discrimination victims of AIDS experience—Tom Hanks and Denzel Washington make the story believable)

*Hurricane*
(The true story of boxer Rubin "Hurricane" Carter's fight against an unjust life sentence in prison—Another great performance by Denzel Washington)

*Planes, Trains, and Automobiles*
(Steve Martin and John Candy at their best in a tale about loneliness and misplaced priorities)

*Uncle Buck*
(The story of a loser uncle's transforming impact on his niece and nephew—starring John Candy)

*My Big Fat Greek Wedding*
(Just for fun!)

*It's a Wonderful Life*
(Because it is)

And finally:

*National Lampoon's Christmas Vacation*
(If this one doesn't make you laugh, you probably should quit the ministry!)

# Conclusion: The Need for Fresh Air

Our family was gathered for a holiday dinner. In the midst of the chatter from various conversations going on in the room at the same time, my adult nephew, who at the time was still single, asked his great uncle a question whose answer I will never forget.

"So uncle Edgar, what is the secret of yours and Aunt Vaida's long marriage?"

Without the slightest hesitation he responded, "Fresh air!"

There it is in a nutshell. Fresh air. It's the key to any lasting marriage, between two people or between a minister and the church. So when all else fails, and you're ready to find something else to do or to put in for early retirement, before you do anything, take a walk. Get some fresh air. It just might make you decide the marriage is worth it after all.

# Notes

## Chapter 1
## Remember Who (Okay, Whom) You Work For

[1]Eugene Peterson, *The Christian Century*, March 13–20, 2002: 19.
[2]Ibid.
[3]Michael Slaughter and Warren Bird, *Unlearning Church: Just When You Thought You Had Leadership All Figured Out* (Loveland, Colo.: Group Publishing, 2002), 27.
[4]Elizabeth O'Connor, *Call To Commitment* (New York: Harper & Row, 1963), 62. (This book has been reissued by The Servant Leadership School of The Church of the Savior).

## Chapter 2
## Remember Who (Whom) You Go to Bed With

[1]This survey is available for review at: http://www.pastorsinfocentral.com/formerpastorsquestionnaire.html
[2]Scott Peck, *The Road Less Traveled* (New York: Simon & Schuster, Inc./ Touchstone Books, 1978), 83.

## Chapter 3
## Remember Why You Go to Work

[1]Malcom Warford, "Our Several Callings" (A Foundation Paper on Vocation as a Lifelong Issue for Education published by The Division of Education and Publication, United Church Board for Homeland Ministries, 1990), 7.
[2]Ibid., 10.
[3]Dallas Willard, *Renovation of the Heart: Putting on The Character of Christ* (Colorado Springs: NavPress, 2002), 55.

## Chapter 4
## Don't Pretend to Know More Than You Do

[1]This telecast was shown during the week of the one-year anniversary of the September 11 attacks and is available for purchase on the PBS Web site, www.pbs.org.

## Chapter 7
## Don't Undervalue Your Influence

[1]The article available through www.startribune.com, is included here in its entirety:
Enough is enough. When Jerry Falwell declares on national television (*60 Minutes*, Oct.6) that Muhammad was a terrorist and Christians believe there will be no peace in Jerusalem until the second coming of Jesus, the time for silence on such religious arrogance is over. Put bluntly, the Christian Right Falwell represents is neither. It is not Christian in attitude and actions because both represent what Jesus spoke and acted against. The Christian Right are the Pharisees of today's Christianity. They play the role of moral and thought police who condemn to hell anyone whose actions they consider wrong and

whose views are different from their own. Their religiosity runs a mile wide but their spirituality is an inch deep.

The Christian Right is not right because it is intellectually dishonest. Falwell speaks as if he knows the Bible when what he actually knows is that which he already believes and imposes on the Bible. He doesn't interpret the Book of Revelation which he claims is the basis for his views on the Middle East, the fate of the world, the second coming of Jesus, and just about anything else he says he believes. Instead, he espouses the views of a man named John Darby whose interpretation of Revelation was popularized by the Scofield Bible in the 19th century. That's where Falwell and his Christian Right still live—in the 19th century when a triumphal Christianity preached a message of oppressive legalism.

The news media love to put Falwell and his kind on national television because it creates conflict. It also makes Christianity look bad. Through the years we have tried to ignore this man and others like him who are an embarrassment to many of us who claim the Christian tradition as our own. But their views have won a large following among Christians who either refuse to think for themselves or who have been duped into believing Christian Right leaders speak from understanding. They don't. Their views represent religious prejudice that draws lines in the sand that separate people into opposing camps and sows the seeds of hatred, suspicion, and war.

Those of us who are the Christians the Christian Right loves to hate have been silent for too long. In the name of tolerance we have allowed Christianity's most radical believers to turn faith into a cover for self-righteous and love into a sword for divisiveness. It is little wonder that Christianity is in decline in America. In our view the Christian Right gives new meaning to Gandhi's comment that he might have become a Christian had he not known so many.

We confess that we have been timid to say openly that the way the Christian Right reads the Bible has at the least no credibility and at worst is patently dishonest. The moment anyone declares the Bible says, they are misrepresenting truth. The Bible doesn't say anything. Every translation is an interpretation and every preacher is an interpreter of that interpretation. So what we say the Bible says is what we have interpreted the Bible to say. To pretend otherwise is to claim knowledge not even the biblical writers claim for themselves. Even more, it ignores what any good biblical student should know, namely, that in the Bible itself there are contrasting interpretations of the ways of God, as for example the Book of Job's rejection of the Deuteronomic ethic that claims God rewards the faithful and punishes the unfaithful

We believe the Christian Right have every right to disagree with us. They have every right to believe we are misguided in what we believe. What they do not have the right to do is to speak as if they speak for God. They do not have the right to presume that their minds are not subject to the fallibility that inflicts the rest of us. They do not have the right to claim that their views represent true Christianity and any other is condemned by God.

Americans believe all people have a right to their views. We couldn't agree more. Sadly and tragically, the Christian Right do not. That is why enough is enough!

# Chapter 10
## Don't Idealize Motivation

[1]Dietrich Bonhoeffer, *Life Together* (New York: Harper & Row, 1954), 26–27.

# Chapter 11
## Don't Try to Leap Tall Buidings in a Single Bound

[1]To see the entire document, contact the group at the following Web site: www.docclimatechange.org

[2]James P. Wind and Gilbert R. Rendle, eds., *The Leadership Situation Facing American Congregations* (Bethesda, Md.: Alban Institute, 2003), 13.

## Chapter 14
## Show Gratitude to the People Who Love You

[1]M. J. Ryan, *Attitudes of Gratitude* (New York: MJF Books, 1999), 6.
[2]Ibid., 68.
[3]Ibid., 69.

## Chapter 16
## Use Your Ears as Well as Your Mouth

[1]Patrick Henry, *The Ironic Christian's Companion* (New York: Riverhead Books, 1999), 153.
[2]Ibid., 154.

## Chapter 18
## Know When to Hold Firm

[1]Martin Luther King, Jr., *Strength To Love* (New York: Harper & Row, 1963), 43.
[2]Ibid.

## Chapter 20
## Know the Difference Between Pointing and Pushing

[1]Robert Greenleaf, "The Servant As Leader" (Cambridge, Mass.: Center for Applied Studies, 1970), 9.
[2]Elton Trueblood, *The Incendiary Fellowship* (New York: Harper & Row, 1967), 43.
[3]Ibid., 44.

## Chapter 21
## Know When to Walk a Thin Line without Drawing One in the Sand

[1]Elton Trueblood, *The Incendiary Fellowship* (New York: Harper & Row, 1967), 45.
[2]Jan Linn, *How to Be an Open-Minded Christian without Losing Your Faith* (St. Louis: Chalice Press, 2001).